THE ARMIES OF LABOR

TEXTBOOK EDITION

∴

THE YALE CHRONICLES
OF AMERICA SERIES

ALLEN JOHNSON

EDITOR

GERHARD R. LOMER
CHARLES W. JEFFERYS

ASSISTANT EDITORS

THE
ARMIES OF LABOR

A CHRONICLE OF THE
ORGANIZED WAGE-EARNERS
BY SAMUEL P. ORTH

TORONTO: GLASGOW, BROOK & CO.
NEW YORK: UNITED STATES PUBLISHERS
ASSOCIATION, INC.

Printed in the United States of America

CONTENTS

THE ARMIES OF LABOR

CHAPTER I

THE BACKGROUND

THREE momentous things symbolize the era that begins its cycle with the memorable year of 1776: the Declaration of Independence, the steam engine, and Adam Smith's book, *The Wealth of Nations*. The Declaration gave birth to a new nation, whose millions of acres of free land were to shift the economic equilibrium of the world; the engine multiplied man's productivity a thousandfold and uprooted in a generation the customs of centuries; the book gave to statesmen a new view of economic affairs and profoundly influenced the course of international trade relations.

The American people, as they faced the approaching age with the experiences of the race behind them, fashioned many of their institutions and laws on British models.   This is true to such an extent that the subject of this book, the rise of labor in America, cannot be understood without a preliminary survey of the British industrial system nor even without some reference to the feudal system, of which English society for many centuries bore the marks and to which many relics of tenure and of class and governmental responsibility may be traced.   Feudalism was a society in which the status of an individual was fixed: he was underman or overman in a rigid social scale according as he considered his relation to his superiors or to his inferiors.   Whatever movement there was took place horizontally, in the same class or on the same social level.   The movement was not vertical, as it so frequently is today, and men did not ordinarily rise above the social level of their birth, never by design, and only perhaps by rare accident or genius.   It was a little world of lords and serfs: of knights who graced court and castle, jousted at tournaments, or fought upon the field of battle; and of serfs who toiled in the fields, served in the castle, or, as the retainers of the knight, formed the crude soldiery of medieval days.   For their labor and allegiance they were clothed and housed and fed.   Yet though there were feast days gay with the color of pageantry and procession, the worker was always in a servile state, an underman dependent upon his master, and sometimes looking upon his condition as little better than slavery.

With the break-up of this rigid system came in England the emancipation of the serf, the rise of the artisan class, and the beginnings of peasant agriculture. That personal gravitation which always draws together men of similar ambitions and tasks now began to work significant changes in the economic order. The peasantry, more or less scattered in the country, found it difficult to unite their powers for redressing their grievances, although there were some peasant revolts of no mean proportions. But the artisans of the towns were soon grouped into powerful organizations, called guilds, so carefully managed and so well disciplined that they dominated every craft and controlled every detail in every trade. The relation of master to journeyman and apprentice, the wages, hours, quantity, and quality of the output, were all minutely regulated. Merchant guilds, similarly constituted, also prospered. The magnificent guild halls that remain in our day are monuments of the power and splendor of these organizations that made the towns of the later Middle Ages flourishing

centers of trade, of handicrafts, and of art. As
towns developed, they dealt the final blow to an
agricultural system based on feudalism: they became cities of refuge for the runaway serfs, and
their charters, insuring political and economic freedom, gave them superior advantages for trading.

The guild system of manufacture was gradually
replaced by the domestic system. The workman's
cottage, standing in its garden, housed the loom
and the spinning wheel, and the entire family was
engaged in labor at home. But the workman,
thus apparently independent, was not the owner of
either the raw material or the finished product. A
middleman or agent brought him the wool, carried
away the cloth, and paid him his hire. Daniel
Defoe, who made a tour of Britain in 1724–6, left
a picture of rural England in this period, often
called the golden age of labor. The land, he says,
"was divided into small inclosures from two acres
to six or seven each, seldom more: every three or
four pieces of land had an house belonging to them,
. . . hardly an house standing out of a speaking
distance from another. . . . We could see at every
house a tenter, and on almost every tenter a piece
of cloth or kersie or shalloon. . . . At every considerable house was a manufactory. . . . **Every**

clothier keeps one horse, at least, to carry his manu-
factures to the market and every one generally
keeps a cow or two or more for his family. By this
means the small pieces of inclosed land about each
house are occupied, for they scarce sow corn enough
to feed their poultry. . . . The houses are full of
lusty fellows, some at the dye vat, some at the
looms, others dressing the clothes; the women or
children carding or spinning, being all employed,
from the youngest to the oldest."

But more significant than these changes was
the rise of the so-called mercantile system, in which
the state took under its care industrial details that
were formerly regulated by the town or guild.
This system, beginning in the sixteenth century
and lasting through the eighteenth, had for its
prime object the upbuilding of national trade.
The state, in order to insure the homogeneous
development of trade and industry, dictated the
prices of commodities. It prescribed the laws of
apprenticeship and the rules of master and servant.
It provided inspectors for passing on the quality
of goods offered for sale. It weighed the loaves,
measured the cloth, and tested the silverware. It
prescribed wages, rural and urban, and bade the
local justice act as a sort of guardian over the

laborers in his district. To relieve poverty poor laws were passed; to prevent the decline of productivity corn laws were passed fixing arbitrary prices for grain. For a time monopolies creating artificial prosperity were granted to individuals and to corporations for the manufacture, sale, or exploitation of certain articles, such as matches, gunpowder, and playing-cards.

This highly artificial and paternalistic state was not content with regulating all these internal matters but spread its protection over foreign commerce. Navigation acts attempted to monopolize the trade of the colonies and especially the trade in the products needed by the mother country. England encouraged shipping and during this period achieved that dominance of the sea which has been the mainstay of her vast empire. She fostered plantations and colonies not for their own sake but that they might be tributaries to the wealth of the nation. An absurd importance was attached to the possession of gold and silver, and the ingenuity of statesmen was exhausted in designing lures to entice these metals to London. Banking and insurance began to assume prime importance. By 1750 England had sent ships into every sea and had planted colonies around the globe.

But while the mechanism of trade and of government made surprising progress during the mercantile period, the mechanism of production remained in the slow handicraft stage. This was now to change. In 1738 Kay invented the flying shuttle, multiplying the capacity of the loom. In 1767 Hargreaves completed the spinning-jenny, and in 1771 Arkwright perfected his roller spinning machine. A few years later Crompton combined the roller and the jenny, and after the application of steam to spinning in 1785 the power loom replaced the hand loom. The manufacture of woolen cloth being the principal industry of England, it was natural that machinery should first be invented for the spinning and weaving of wool. New processes in the manufacture of iron and steel and the development of steam transportation soon followed.

Within the course of a few decades the whole economic order was changed. Whereas many centuries had been required for the slow development of the medieval system of feudalism, the guild system, and the handicrafts, now, like a series of earthquake shocks, came changes so sudden and profound that even today society has not yet learned to adjust itself to the myriads of needs and possibilities which the union of man's mind with nature's forces has produced. The industrial revolution took the workman from the land and crowded him into the towns. It took the loom from his cottage and placed it in the factory. It took the tool from his hand and harnessed it to a shaft. It robbed him of his personal skill and joined his arm of flesh to an arm of iron. It reduced him from a craftsman to a specialist, from a maker of shoes to a mere stitcher of soles. It took from him, at a single blow, his interest in the workmanship of his task, his ownership of the tools, his garden, his wholesome environment, and even his family. All were swallowed by the black maw of the ugly new mill town. The hardships of the old days were soon forgotten in the horrors of the new. For the transition was rapid enough to make the contrast striking. Indeed it was so rapid that the new class of employers, the capitalists, found little time to think of anything but increasing their profits, and the new class of employees, now merely wage-earners, found that their long hours of monotonous toil gave them little leisure and no interest.

The transition from the age of handicrafts to the era of machines presents a picture of greed that tempts one to bitter invective. Its details are dispassionately catalogued by the Royal Commissions that finally towards the middle of the nineteenth century inquired into industrial conditions. From these reports Karl Marx drew inspiration for his social philosophy, and in them his friend Engles found the facts that he retold so vividly, for the purpose of arousing his fellow workmen. And Carlyle and Ruskin, reading this official record of selfishness, and knowing its truth, drew their powerful indictments against a society which would permit its eight-year-old daughters, its mothers, and its grandmothers, to be locked up for fourteen hours a day in dirty, ill-smelling factories, to release them at night only to find more misery in the hovels they pitifully called home.

The introduction of machinery into manufacturing wrought vast changes also in the organization of business. The unit of industry greatly increased in size. The economies of organized wholesale production were soon made apparent; and the tendency to increase the size of the factory and to amalgamate the various branches of industry under corporate control has continued to the present. The complexity of business operations also increased with the development of transportation

and the expansion of the empire of trade. A
world market took the place of the old town market,
and the world market necessitated credit on a new
and infinitely larger scale.

No less important than the revolution in industry was the revolution in economic theory which
accompanied it. Unlimited competition replaced
the state paternalism of the mercantilists. Adam
Smith in 1776 espoused the cause of economic liberty, believing that if business and industry were
unhampered by artificial restrictions they would
work out their own salvation. His pronouncement
was scarcely uttered before it became the shibboleth of statesmen and business men. The revolt
of the American colonies hastened the general acceptance of this doctrine, and England soon found
herself committed to the practice of every man
looking after his own interests. Freedom of contract, freedom of trade, and freedom of thought
were vigorous and inspiring but often misleading
phrases. The processes of specialization and centralization that were at work portended the growing power of those who possessed the means to
build factories and ships and railways but not nec-
essarily the freedom of the many. The doctrine of
laissez faire assumed that power would bring with

it a sense of responsibility. For centuries, the old-country gentry and governing class of England had shown an appreciation of their duties, as a class, to those dependent upon them. But now another class with no benevolent traditions of responsibility came into power — the capitalist, a parvenu whose ambition was profit, not equity, and whose dealings with other men were not tempered by the amenities of the gentleman but were sharpened by the necessities of gain. It was upon such a class, new in the economic world and endowed with astounding power, that Adam Smith's new formularies of freedom were let loose.

During all these changes in the economic order, the interest of the laborer centered in one question: What return would he receive for his toil? With the increasing complexity of society, many other problems presented themselves to the worker, but for the most part they were subsidiary to the main question of wages. As long as man's place was fixed by law or custom, a customary wage left small margin for controversy. But when fixed status gave way to voluntary contract, when payment was made in money, when workmen were free to journey from town to town, labor became both free and fluid, bargaining took the place of custom, and the wage controversy began to assume definite proportions. As early as 1348 the great plague became a landmark in the field of wage disputes. So scarce had laborers become through the ravages of the Black Death, that wages rose rapidly, to the alarm of the employers, who prevailed upon King Edward III to issue the historic proclamation of 1349, directing that no laborer should demand and no employer should pay greater wages than those customary before the plague. This early attempt to outmaneuver an economic law by a legal device was only the prelude to a long series of labor laws which may be said to have culminated in the great Statute of Laborers of 1562, regulating the relations of wage-earner and employer and empowering justices of the peace to fix the wages in their districts. Wages steadily decreased during the two hundred years in which this statute remained in force, and poor laws were passed to bring the succor which artificial wages made necessary. Thus two rules of arbitrary government were meant to neutralize each other. It is the usual verdict of historians that the estate of labor in England declined from a flourishing condition in the fourteenth and fifteenth centuries to one of great distress by the time of the Industrial

Revolution. This unhappy decline was probably due to several causes, among which the most important were the arbitrary and artificial attempts of the Government to keep down wages, the heavy taxation caused by wars of expansion, and the want of coercive power on the part of labor.

From the decline of the guild system, which had placed labor and its products so completely in the hands of the master craftsman, the workman had assumed no controlling part in the labor bargain. Such guilds and such journeyman's fraternities as may have survived were practically helpless against parliamentary rigor and state benevolence. In the domestic stage of production, cohesion among workers was not so necessary. But when the factory system was substituted for the handi-craft system and workers with common interests were thrown together in the towns, they had every impulsion towards organization. They not only felt the need of sociability after long hours spent in spiritless toil but they were impelled by a new consciousness — the realization that an inevitable and profound change had come over their condition. They had ceased to be journeymen controlling in some measure their activities: they were now merely wage-earners. As the realization of this adverse change came over them, they began to resent the unsanitary and burdensome conditions under which they were compelled to live and to work.   So actual grievances were added to fear of what might happen, and in their common cause experience soon taught them unity of action.   Parliament was petitioned, agitations were organized, sick-benefits were inaugurated, and when these methods failed, machinery was destroyed, factories were burned, and the strike became a common weapon of self-defense.

Though a few labor organizations can be traced as far back as 1700, their growth during the eighteenth century was slow and irregular.   There was no unity in their methods, and they were known by many names, such as associations, unions, union societies, trade clubs, and trade societies.   These societies had no legal status and their meetings were usually held in secret.   And the Webbs in their *History of Trade Unionism* allude to the traditions of "the midnight meeting of patriots in the corner of the field, the buried box of records, the secret oath, the long terms of imprisonment of the leading officials."   Some of these tales were unquestionably apocryphal, others were exaggerated by feverish repetition.   But they indicate

the aversion with which the authorities looked
upon these combinations.

There were two legal doctrines long invoked by
the English courts against combined action — doctrines that became a heritage of the United States
and have had a profound effect upon the labor
movements in America. The first of these was the
doctrine of conspiracy, a doctrine so ancient that
its sources are obscure. It was the natural product of a government and of a time that looked
askance at all combined action, fearing sedition,
intrigue, and revolution. As far back as 1305
there was enacted a statute defining conspiracy and
outlining the offense. It did not aim at any definite social class but embraced all persons who combined for a "malicious enterprise." Such an enterprise was the breaking of a law. So when Parliament passed acts regulating wages, conditions of
employment, or prices of commodities, those who
combined secretly or openly to circumvent the act,
to raise wages or lower them, or to raise prices and
curtail markets, at once fell under the ban of conspiracy. The law operated alike on conspiring
employers and conniving employees.

The new class of employers during the early
years of the machine age eagerly embraced the

doctrine of conspiracy. They readily brought under the legal definition the secret connivings of the wage-earners. Political conditions now also worked against the laboring class. The unrest in the colonies that culminated in the independence of America and the fury of the French Revolution combined to make kings and aristocracies wary of all organizations and associations of plain folk And when we add to this the favor which the new employing class, the industrial masters, were able to extort from the governing class, because of their power over foreign trade and domestic finance, we can understand the compulsory laws at length declaring against all combinations of working men.

The second legal doctrine which Americans have inherited from England and which has played a leading rôle in labor controversies is the doctrine that declares unlawful all combinations in restraint of trade. Like its twin doctrine of conspiracy, it is of remote historical origin. One of the earliest uses, perhaps the first use, of the term by Parliament was in the statute of 1436 forbidding guilds and trading companies from adopting by-laws "in restraint of trade," and forbidding practices in price manipulations "for their own profit and to the common hurt of the people." This doctrine thus early invoked, and repeatedly reasserted against combinations of traders and masters, was incorporated in the general statute of 1800 which declared all combinations of journeymen illegal. But in spite of legal doctrines, of innumerable laws and court decisions, strikes and combinations multiplied, and devices were found for evading statutory wages.

In 1824 an act of Parliament removed the general prohibition of combinations and accorded to workingmen the right to bargain collectively. Three men were responsible for this noteworthy reform, each one a new type in British politics. The first was Francis Place, a tailor who had taken active part in various strikes. He was secretary of the London Corresponding Society, a powerful labor union, which in 1795 had twenty branches in London. Most of the officers of this organization were at one time or another arrested, and some were kept in prison three years without a trial. Place, schooled in such experience, became a radical politician of great influence, a friend of Bentham, Owen, and the elder Mill. The second type of new reformer was represented by Joseph Hume, a physician who had accumulated wealth in the India Service, who had returned home to enter public life, and who was converted from Toryism to

Radicalism by a careful study of financial, political, and industrial problems. A great number of reform laws can be traced directly to his incredible activity during his thirty years in Parliament. The third leader was John R. McCulloch, an orthodox economist, a disciple of Adam Smith, for some years editor of *The Scotsman*, which was then a violently radical journal coöperating with the newly established *Edinburgh Review* in advocating sociological and political reforms.

Thus Great Britain, the mother country from which Americans have inherited so many institutions, laws, and traditions, passed in turn through the periods of extreme paternalism, glorified competition, and governmental antagonism to labor combinations, into what may be called the age of conciliation. And today the Labour Party in the House of Commons has shown itself strong enough to impose its programme upon the Liberals and, through this radical coalition, has achieved a power for the working man greater than even Francis Place or Thomas Carlyle ever hoped for.

CHAPTER II

FORMATIVE YEARS

AMERICA did not become a cisatlantic Britain, as some of the colonial adventurers had hoped. A wider destiny awaited her. Here were economic conditions which upset all notions of the fixity of class distinctions. Here was a continent of free land, luring the disaffected or disappointed artisan and enabling him to achieve economic independence. Hither streamed ceaselessly hordes of immigrants from Europe, constantly shifting the social equilibrium. Here the demand for labor was constant, except during the rare intervals of financial stagnation, and here the door of opportunity swung wide to the energetic and able artisan. The records of American industry are replete with names of prominent leaders who began at the apprentice's bench.

The old class distinctions brought from the home country, however, had survived for many years in the primeval forests of Virginia and Maryland and even among the hills of New England. Indeed, until the Revolution and for some time thereafter, a man's clothes were the badge of his calling. The gentleman wore powdered queue and ruffled shirt; the workman, coarse buckskin breeches, ponderous shoes with brass buckles, and usually a leather apron, well greased to keep it pliable. Just before the Revolution the lot of the common laborer was not an enviable one. His house was rude and barren of comforts; his fare was coarse and without variety. His wage was two shillings a day, and prison — usually an indescribably filthy hole — awaited him the moment he ran into debt. The artisan fared somewhat better. He had spent, as a rule, seven years learning his trade, and his skill and energy demanded and generally received a reasonable return. The account books that have come down to us from colonial days show that his handiwork earned him a fair living. This, however, was before machinery had made inroads upon the product of cabinetmaker, tailor, shoemaker, locksmith, and silversmith, and when the main street of every village was picturesque with the signs of the crafts that maintained the decent independence of the community.

Such labor organizations as existed before the Revolution were limited to the skilled trades. In 1648 the coopers and the shoemakers of Boston were granted permission to organize guilds, which embraced both master and journeyman, and there were a few similar organizations in New York, Philadelphia, and Baltimore. But these were not unions like those of today. "There are," says Richard T. Ely, "no traces of anything like a modern trades union in the colonial period of American history, and it is evident on reflection that there was little need, if any, of organization on the part of labor, at that time."[1]

A new epoch for labor came in with the Revolution. Within a decade wages rose fifty per cent, and John Jay in 1784 writes of the "wages of mechanics and laborers" as "very extravagant." Though the industries were small and depended on a local market within a circumscribed area of communication, they grew rapidly. The period following the Revolution is marked by considerable industrial restiveness and by the formation of many labor organizations, which were, however, benevolent or friendly societies rather than unions and were often incorporated by an act of the

[1] *The Labor Movement in America*, by Richard T. Ely (1905), p. 36.

legislature. In New York, between 1800 and 1810, twenty-four such societies were incorporated. Only in the larger cities were they composed of artisans of one trade, such as the New York Masons Society (1807) or the New York Society of Journeymen Shipwrights (1807). Elsewhere they included artisans of many trades, such as the Albany Mechanical Society (1801). In Philadelphia the cordwainers, printers, and hatters had societies. In Baltimore the tailors were the first to organize, and they conducted in 1795 one of the first strikes in America. Ten years later they struck again, and succeeded in raising their pay from seven shillings sixpence the job to eight shillings ninepence and "extras." At the same time the pay of unskilled labor was rising rapidly, for workers were scarce owing to the call of the merchant marine in those years of the rising splendor of the American sailing ship, and the lure of western lands. The wages of common laborers rose to a dollar and more a day.

There occurred in 1805 an important strike of the Philadelphia cordwainers. Theirs was one of the oldest labor organizations in the country, and it had conducted several successful strikes. This particular occasion, however, is significant, because the strikers were tried for conspiracy in the mayor's court, with the result that they were found guilty and fined eight dollars each, with costs. As the court permitted both sides to tell their story in detail, a full report of the proceedings survives to give us, as it were, a photograph of the labor conditions of that time. The trial kindled a great deal of local animosity. A newspaper called the *Aurora* contained inflammatory accounts of the proceedings, and a pamphlet giving the records of the court was widely circulated. This pamphlet bore the significant legend, "It is better that the law be known and certain, than that it be right," and was dedicated to the Governor and General Assembly "with the hope of attracting their particular attention, at the next meeting of the legislature."

Another early instance of a strike occurred in New York City in 1809, when the cordwainers struck for higher wages and were haled before the mayor's court on the charge of conspiracy. The trial was postponed by Mayor DeWitt Clinton until after the pending municipal elections to avoid the risk of offending either side. When at length the strikers were brought to trial, the court-house was crowded with spectators, showing how keen was the public interest in the case. The jury's

verdict of "guilty," and the imposition of a fine of
one dollar each and costs upon the defendants
served but as a stimulus to the friends of the strikers
to gather in a great mass meeting and protest against
the verdict and the law that made it possible.

In 1821 the New York Typographical Society,
which had been organized four years earlier by
Peter Force, a labor leader of unusual energy, set a
precedent for the vigorous and fearless career of
its modern successor by calling a strike in the
printing office of Thurlow Weed, the powerful
politician, himself a member of the society, because he employed a "rat," as a nonunion worker
was called.   It should be noted, however, that the
organizations of this early period were of a loose
structure and scarcely comparable to the labor
unions of today.

Sidney Smith, the brilliant contributor to the
Edinburgh Review, propounded in 1820 certain
questions which sum up the general conditions of
American industry and art after nearly a half
century of independence: "In the four quarters of
the globe," he asked, "who reads an American
book? or goes to an American play? or looks at an
American picture or statue?   What does the world

yet owe to American physicians or surgeons?
What new substances have their chemists discovered? or what old ones have they analyzed?
What new constellations have been discovered by
the telescopes of Americans? What have they
done in mathematics? Who drinks out of American glasses? or eats from American plates? or wears
American coats or gowns? or sleeps in American
blankets?"

These questions, which were quite pertinent,
though conceived in an impertinent spirit, were
being answered in America even while the witty
Englishman was framing them. The water power
of New England was being harnessed to cotton
mills, woolen mills, and tanneries. Massachusetts in 1820 reported one hundred and sixty-one
factories. New York had begun that marvelous
growth which made the city, in the course of a few
decades, the financial capital of a hemisphere. So
rapidly were people flocking to New York, that
houses had tenants long before they had windows
and doors, and streets were lined with buildings
before they had sewers, sidewalks, or pavements.
New Jersey had well under way those manufacto-
ries of glassware, porcelains, carpets, and textiles
which have since brought her great prosperity.

Philadelphia was the country's greatest weaving center, boasting four thousand craftsmen engaged in that industry. Even on the frontier, Pittsburgh and Cincinnati were emerging from "settlements" into manufacturing towns of importance. McMaster concludes his graphic summary of these years as follows: "In 1820 it was estimated that 200,000 persons and a capital of $75,000,000 were employed in manufacturing. In 1825 the capital used had been expanded to $160,000,000 and the number of workers to 2,000,000."[1]

The Industrial Revolution had set in. These new millions who hastened to answer the call of industry in the new land were largely composed of the poor of other lands. Thousands of them were paupers when they landed in America, their passage having been paid by those at home who wanted to get rid of them. Vast numbers settled down in the cities, in spite of the lure of the land. It was at this period that universal manhood suffrage was written into the constitutions of the older States, and a new electorate assumed the reins of power. Now the first labor representatives were sent to the legislatures and to Congress, and the older parties began eagerly bidding for the votes of the

[1] *History of the People of the United States* (1901), vol. v, p. 230.

humble. The decision of great questions fell to this new electorate. With the rise of industry came the demand for a protective tariff and for better transportation. State governments vied with each other, in thoughtless haste, in lending their credit to new turnpike and canal construction. And above all political issues loomed the Bank, the monopoly that became the laborer's bugaboo and Andrew Jackson's opportunity to rally to his side the newly enfranchised mechanics.

So the old days of semi-colonial composure were succeeded by the thrilling experiences that a new industrial prosperity thrusts upon a really democratic electorate. Little wonder that the labor union movement took the political by-path, seeking salvation in the promise of the politician and in the panacea of fatuous laws. Now there were to be discerned the beginnings of class solidarity among the working people. But the individual's chances to improve his situation were still very great and opportunity was still a golden word.

The harsh facts of the hour, however, soon began to call for united action. The cities were expanding with such eager haste that proper housing conditions were overlooked. Workingmen were obliged to live in wretched structures. Moreover, human beings were still levied on for debt and imprisoned for default of payment. Children of less than sixteen years of age were working twelve or more hours a day, and if they received any education at all, it was usually in schools charitably called "ragged schools" or "poor schools," or "pauper schools." There was no adequate redress for the mechanic if his wages were in default, for lien laws had not yet found their way into the statute books. Militia service was oppressive, permitting only the rich to buy exemption. It was still considered an unlawful conspiracy to act in unison for an increase in pay or a lessening of working hours. By 1840 the pay of unskilled labor had dropped to about seventy-five cents a day in the overcrowded cities, and in the winter, in either city or country, many unskilled workers were glad to work for merely their board. The lot of women workers was especially pitiful. A seamstress by hard toil, working fifteen hours a day might stitch enough shirts to earn from seventy-two cents to a dollar and twelve cents a week. Skilled labor, while faring better in wages, shared with the unskilled in the universal working day which lasted from sun to sun. Such in brief were the conditions that brought home to the laboring masses that homogeneous consciousness which alone makes a group powerful in a democracy.

The movement can most clearly be discerned in the cities. Philadelphia claims precedence as the home of the first Trades' Union. The master cordwainers had organized a society in 1792, and their journeymen had followed suit two years later. The experiences and vicissitudes of these shoemakers furnished a useful lesson to other tradesmen, many of whom were organized into unions. But they were isolated organizations, each one fighting its own battles. In 1827 the Mechanics' Union of Trade Associations was formed. Of its significance John R. Commons says:

England is considered the home of trade-unionism, but the distinction belongs to Philadelphia. . . . The first trades' union in England was that of Manchester, organized in 1829, although there seems to have been an attempt to organize one in 1824. But the first one in America was the "Mechanics' Union of Trade Associations," organized in Philadelphia in 1827, two years earlier. The name came from Manchester, but the thing from Philadelphia. Neither union lasted long. The Manchester union lived two years, and the Philadelphia union one year. But the Manchester union died and the Philadelphia union metamorphosed into politics. Here again Philadelphia was the pioneer, for it called into being the first labor party. Not

only this, but through the Mechanics' Union Philadelphia started probably the first wage-earners' paper
ever published — the *Mechanics Free Press* — ante-
dating, in January, 1828, the first similar journal in
England by two years.[1]

The union had its inception in the first general
building strike called in America.   In the summer
of 1827 the carpenters struck for a ten-hour day.
They were soon joined by the bricklayers, painters,
and glaziers, and members of other trades.   But
the strike failed of its immediate object.   A second
effort to combine the various trades into one organization was made in 1833, when the Trades' Union
of the City and County of Philadelphia, was formed.
Three years later this union embraced some fifty
societies with over ten thousand members.   In
June, 1835, this organization undertook what was
probably the first successful general strike in America.   It began among the cordwainers, spread to
the workers in the building trades, and was presently joined in by cigarmakers, carters, saddlers
and harness makers, smiths, plumbers, bakers,
printers, and even by the unskilled workers on the
docks.   The strikers' demand for a ten-hour day received a great deal of support from the influential

[1] *Labor Organization and Labor Politics, 1827–37;* in the *Quarterly
Journal of Economics*, February, 1907.

men in the community.   After a mass meeting of
citizens had adopted resolutions endorsing the
demands of the union, the city council agreed to
a ten-hour day for all municipal employees.

In 1833 the carpenters of New York City struck
for an increase in wages.   They were receiving a
dollar thirty-seven and a half cents a day; they
asked for a dollar and a half.   They obtained the
support of other workers, notably the tailors,
printers, brushmakers, tobacconists, and masons,
and succeeded in winning their strike in one month.
The printers, who have always been alert and active in New York City, elated by the success of
this coördinate effort, sent out a circular calling
for a general convention of all the trades societies
of the city.   After a preliminary meeting in July,
a mass meeting was held in December, at which
there were present about four thousand persons
representing twenty-one societies.   The outcome
of the meeting was the organization of the General
Trades' Union of New York City.

It happened in the following year that Ely
Moore of the Typographical Association and the
first president of the new union, a powerful ora-
tor and a sagacious organizer, was elected to Congress on the Jackson ticket.   He was backed by

Tammany Hall, always on the alert for winners, and was supported by the mechanics, artisans, and workingmen. He was the first man to take his seat in Washington as the avowed representative of labor.

The movement for a ten-hour day was now in full swing, and the years 1834–7 were full of strikes. The most spectacular of these struggles was the strike of the tailors of New York in 1836, in the course of which twenty strikers were arrested for conspiracy. After a spirited trial attended by throngs of spectators, the men were found guilty by a jury which took only thirty minutes for deliberation. The strikers were fined $50 each, except the president of the society, who was fined $150. After the trial there was held a mass meeting which was attended, according to the *Evening Post*, by twenty-seven thousand persons. Resolutions were passed declaring that "to all acts of tyranny and injustice, resistance is just and therefore necessary," and "that the construction given to the law in the case of the journeymen tailors is not only ridiculous and weak in practice but unjust in principle and subversive of the rights and liberties of American citizens." The town was placarded with "coffin" handbills, a practice not uncommon in those days.

Enclosed in a device representing a coffin were these words:

THE RICH AGAINST THE POOR!

Twenty of your brethren have been found guilty for presuming to resist a reduction in their wages! . . . Judge Edwards has charged . . . the Rich are the only judges of the wants of the poor.   On Monday, June 6, 1836, the Freemen are to receive their sentence, to gratify the hellish appetites of aristocracy! . . .   Go! Go! Go! Every Freeman, every Workingman, and hear the melancholy sound of the earth on the Coffin of Equality. Let the Court Room, the City-hall — yea, the whole Park, be filled with mourners! But remember, offer no violence to Judge Edwards! Bend meekly and receive the chains wherewith you are to be bound! Keep the peace! Above all things, keep the peace!

The *Evening Post* concludes a long account of the affair by calling attention to the fact that the Trades Union was not composed of "only foreigners."   "It is a low calculation when we estimate that two-thirds of the workingmen of the city, numbering several thousand persons, belong to it," and that "it is controlled and supported by the great majority of our native born."

The Boston Trades Union was organized in 1834 and started out with a great labor parade on the

Fourth of July, followed by a dinner served to a thousand persons in Faneuil Hall. This union was formed primarily to fight for the ten-hour day, and the leading crusaders were the house carpenters, the ship carpenters, and the masons. Similar unions presently sprang up in other cities, including Baltimore, Albany, Troy, Washington, Newark, Schenectady, New Brunswick, Pittsburgh, Cincinnati, and St. Louis. By 1835 all the larger centers of industry were familiar with the idea, and most of them with the practice, of the trades organizations of a community uniting for action.

The local unions were not unmindful of the need for wider action, either through a national union of all the organizations of a single trade, or through a union of all the different trades unions. Both courses of action were attempted. In 1834 the National Trades Union came into being and from that date held annual national conventions of all the trades until the panic of 1837 obliterated the movement. When the first convention was called, it was estimated that there were some 26,250 members of trades unions then in the United States. Of these 11,500 were in New York and its vicinity, 6000 in Philadelphia, 4000 in Boston, and 3500 in Baltimore. Meanwhile a movement was under way to federate the unions of a single trade. In 1835 the cordwainers attending the National Trades Union formed a preliminary organization and called a national cordwainers' convention. This met in New York in March, 1836, and included forty-five delegates from New York, New Jersey, Delaware, and Connecticut. In the fall of 1836 the comb-makers, the carpenters, the hand-loom weavers, and the printers likewise organized separate national unions or alliances, and several other trades made tentative efforts by correspondence to organize themselves in the same manner.

Before the dire year of 1837, there are, then, to be found the beginnings of most of the elements of modern labor organizations — benevolent societies and militant orders; political activities and trades activities; amalgamations of local societies of the same trades and of all trades; attempts at national organization on the part of both the local trades unions and of the local trade unions; a labor press to keep alive the interest of the workman; mass meetings, circulars, conventions, and appeals to arouse the interest of the public in the issues of the hour. The persistent demand of the workingmen was for a ten-hour day. Harriet Martineau, who

traveled extensively through the United States, remarked that all the strikes she heard of were on
the question of hours, not wages. But there were
nevertheless abundant strikes either to raise wages
or to maintain them. There were, also, other
fundamental questions in controversy which could
not be settled by strikes, such as imprisonment for
debt, lien and exemption and homestead laws,
convict labor and slave labor, and universal education. Most of these issues have since that time
been decided in favor of labor, and a new series
of demands takes their place today. Yet as one
reads the records of the early conspiracy cases or
thumbs through the files of old periodicals, he
learns that there is indeed nothing new under the
sun and that, while perhaps the particular issues
have changed, the general methods and the spirit
of the contest remain the same.

The laborer believed then, as he does now, that
his organization must be all-embracing. In those
days also there were "scabs," often called "rats"
or "dung." Places under ban were systematically
picketed, and warnings like the following were sent
out: "We would caution all strangers and others
who profess the art of horseshoeing, that if they go
to work for any employer under the above prices,

they must abide by the consequences." Usually the consequences were a fine imposed by the union, but sometimes they were more severe. Coercion by the union did not cease with the strike. Journeymen who were not members were pursued with assiduity and energy as soon as they entered a town and found work. The boycott was a method early used against prison labor. New York stonecutters agreed that they would not "either collectively or individually purchase any goods manufactured" by convicts and that they would not "countenance" any merchants who dealt in them; and employers who incurred the displeasure of organized labor were "nullified."

The use of the militia during strikes presented the same difficulties then as now. During the general strike in Philadelphia in 1835 there was considerable rowdyism, and Michel Chevalier, a keen observer of American life, wrote that "the militia looks on; the sheriff stands with folded hands." Nor was there any difference in the attitude of the laboring man towards unfavorable court decisions. In the tailors' strike in New York in 1836, for instance, twenty-seven thousand sympathizers assembled with bands and banners to protest against the jury's verdict, and after sentence had been imposed upon the defendants, the lusty throng burned the judge in effigy.

Sabotage is a new word, but the practice itself is old. In 1835 the striking cabinet-makers in New York smashed thousands of dollars' worth of chairs, tables, and sofas that had been imported from France, and the newspapers observed the significant fact that the destroyers boasted in a foreign language that only American-made furniture should be sold in America. Houses were burned in Philadelphia because the contractors erecting them refused to grant the wages that were demanded. Vengeance was sometimes sought against new machinery that displaced hand labor. In June, 1835, a New York paper remarked that "it is well known that many of the most obstinate turn-outs among workingmen and many of the most violent and lawless proceedings have been excited for the purpose of destroying newly invented machinery." Such acts of wantonness, however, were few, even in those first tumultuous days of the thirties. Striking became in those days a sort of mania, and not a town that had a mill or shop was exempt. Men struck for "grog or death," for "Liberty, Equality, and the Rights of Man," and even for the right to smoke their pipes at work.

Strike benefits, too, were known in this early period. Strikers in New York received assistance from Philadelphia, and Boston strikers were similarly aided by both New York and Philadelphia. When the high cost of living threatened to deprive the wage-earner of half his income, bread riots occurred in the cities, and handbills circulated in New York bore the legend:

BREAD, MEAT, RENT, FUEL
THEIR PRICES MUST COME DOWN

CHAPTER III

WITH the panic of 1837 the mills were closed, thousands of unemployed workers were thrown upon private charity, and, in the long years of depression which followed, trade unionism suffered a temporary eclipse. It was a period of social unrest in which all sorts of philanthropic reforms were suggested and tried out. Measured by later events, it was a period of transition, of social awakening, of aspiration tempered by the bitter experience of failure.

In the previous decade Robert Owen, the distinguished English social reformer and philanthropist, had visited America and had begun in 1826 his famous colony at New Harmony, Indiana. His experiments at New Lanark, in England, had already made him known to working people the world over. Whatever may be said of his quaint attempts to reduce society to a common denominator, it is certain that his arrival in America, at a time when people's minds were open to all sorts of economic suggestions, had a stimulating effect upon labor reforms and led, in the course of time, to the founding of some forty communistic colonies, most of them in New York, Pennsylvania, and Ohio. "We are all a little wild here with numberless projects of social reform," wrote Emerson to Thomas Carlyle; "not a reading man but has the draft of a new community in his waistcoat pocket." One of these experiments, at Red Bank, New Jersey, lasted for thirteen years, and another, in Wisconsin, for six years. But most of them after a year or two gave up the struggle.

Of these failures, the best known is Brook Farm, an intellectual community founded in 1841 by George Ripley at West Roxbury, Massachusetts. Six years later the project was abandoned and is now remembered as an example of the futility of trying to leaven a world of realism by means of an atom of transcendental idealism. In a sense, however, Brook Farm typifies this period of transition. It was a time of vagaries and longings. People seemed to be conscious of the fact that a new social solidarity was dawning. It is not strange, therefore, that — while the railroads were feeling their way from town to town and across the prairies, while water-power and steam-power were multiplying man's productivity, indicating that the old days were gone forever — many curious dreams of a new order of things should be dreamed, nor that among them some should be ridiculous, some fantastic, and some unworthy, nor that, as the futility of a universal social reform forced itself upon the dreamers, they merged the greater in the lesser, the general in the particular, and sought an outlet in espousing some specific cause or attacking some particular evil.

Those movements which had their inspiration in a genuine humanitarianism achieved great good. Now for the first time the blind, the deaf, the dumb, and the insane were made the object of social solicitude and communal care. The criminal, too, and the jail in which he was confined remained no longer utterly neglected. Men of the debtor class were freed from that medieval barbarism which gave the creditor the right to levy on the person of his debtor. Even the public schools were dragged out of their lethargy. When Horace Mann was appointed secretary of the newly created Massachusetts Board of Education in 1837, a new day dawned for American public schools.

While these and other substantial improvements were under way, the charlatan and the faddist were not without their opportunities or their votaries. Spirit rappings beguiled or awed the villagers; thousands of religious zealots in 1844 abandoned their vocations and, drawing on white robes, awaited expectantly the second coming of Christ: every cult from free love to celibate austerity found zealous followers; the "new woman" declared her independence in short hair and bloomers; people sought so´ ˘ salvation in new health codes, in vegetarian boarding-houses, and in physical culture clul ; and some pursued the way to perfection through sensual religious exercises.

In this seething *milieu*, this medley of practical humanitarianism and social fantasies, the labor movement was revived. In the forties, Thomas Mooney, an observant Irish traveler who had spent several years in the United States wrote as follows[1]:

The average value of a common uneducated labourer is eighty cents a day. Of educated or mechanical labour, one hundred twenty-five and two hundred cents a day; of female labour forty cents a day. Against meat, flour, vegetables, and groceries at

[1] *Nine Years in America* (1850), p. 22.

one-third less than they rate in Great Britain and Ireland; against clothing, house rent and fuel at about equal; against public taxes at about three-fourths less; and a certainty of employment, and a facility of acquiring homes and lands, and education for children, *a hundred to one greater.* The further you penetrate into the country, Patrick, the higher in general will you find the value of labour, and the cheaper the price of all kinds of living. . . . The food of the American farmer, mechanic or labourer is the best I believe enjoyed by any similar classes in the whole world. At every meal there is meat or fish or both; indeed I think the women, children, and sedentary classes eat too much meat for their own good health.

This highly optimistic picture, written by a sanguine observer from the land of greatest agrarian oppression, must be shaded by contrasting details. The truck system of payment, prevalent in mining regions and many factory towns, reduced the actual wage by almost one-half. In the cities, unskilled immigrants had so overcrowded the common labor market that competition had reduced them to a pitiable state. Hours of labor were generally long in the factories. As a rule only the skilled artisan had achieved the ten-hour day, and then only in isolated instances. Woman's labor was the poorest paid, and her condition was the most neglected. A visitor to Lowell in

1846 thus describes the conditions in an average factory of that town:

In Lowell live between seven and eight thousand young women, who are generally daughters of farmers of the different States of New England. Some of them are members of families that were rich the generation before. . . . The operatives work thirteen hours a day in the summer time, and from daylight to dark in the winter. At half-past four in the morning the factory bell rings and at five the girls must be in the mills. A clerk, placed as a watch, observes those who are a few minutes behind the time, and effectual means are taken to stimulate punctuality. . . . At seven the girls are allowed thirty minutes for breakfast, and at noon thirty minutes more for dinner, except during the first quarter of the year, when the time is extended to forty-five minutes. But within this time they must hurry to their boarding-houses and return to the factory. . . . At seven o'clock in the evening the factory bell sounds the close of the day's work.

It was under these conditions that the coöperative movement had its brief day of experiment. As early as 1828 the workmen of Philadelphia and Cincinnati had begun coöperative stores. The Philadelphia group were "fully persuaded," according to their constitution, "that nothing short of an entire change in the present regulation of trade and commerce will ever be permanently beneficial to the productive part of the community." **But** their little shop survived competition for only a few months. The Cincinnati "Coöperative Magazine" was a sort of combination of store and shop, where various trades were taught, but it also soon disappeared.

In 1845 the New England Workingmen's Association organized a protective union for the purpose of obtaining for its members "steady and profitable employment" and of saving the retailer's profit for the purchaser. This movement had a high moral flavor. "The dollar was to us of minor importance; humanitary and not mercenary were our motives," reported their committee on organization of industry. "We must proceed from combined stores to combined shops, from combined shops to combined homes, to joint ownership in God's earth, the foundation that our edifice must stand upon." In this ambitious spirit "they commenced business with a box of soap and half a chest of tea." In 1852 they had 167 branches, a capital of $241,712.66, and a business of nearly $2,000,000 a year.

In the meantime similar coöperative movements began elsewhere. The tailors of Boston struck for higher wages in 1850 and, after fourteen weeks of futile struggle, decided that their salvation lay in coöperation rather than in trade unionism, which at best afforded only temporary relief. About seventy of them raised $700 as a coöperative nest egg and netted a profit of $510.60 the first year. In the same year the Philadelphia printers, disappointed at their failure to force a higher wage, organized a coöperative printing press.

The movement spread to New York, where a strike of the tailors was in progress. The strikers were addressed at a great mass meeting by Albert Brisbane, an ardent disciple of Fourier, the French social economist, and were told that they must do away with servitude to capital. "What we want to know," said Brisbane, "is how to change, peacefully, the system of today. The first great principle is combination." Another meeting was addressed by a German, a follower of Karl Marx, who uttered in his native tongue these words that sound like a modern I. W. W. prophet: "Many of us have fought for liberty in the fatherland. We came here because we were opposed, and what have we gained? Nothing but misery, hunger, and treading down. But we are in a free country and it is our fault if we do not get our rights. . . . Let those who strike eat; the rest starve. Butchers and bakers must withhold supplies. Yes, they must all strike, and then the aristocrat will starve. We must have a revolution. We cannot submit any longer." The cry of "Revolution! Revolution!" was taken up by the throng.

In the midst of this agitation a New York branch of the New England Protective Union was organized as an attempt at peaceful revolution by coöperation. The New York Protective Union went a step farther than the New England Union. Its members established their own shops and so became their own employers. And in many other cities striking workmen and eager reformers joined hands in modest endeavors to change the face of things. The revolutionary movements of Europe at this period were having a seismic effect upon American labor. But all these attempts of the workingmen to tourney a rough world with a needle were foredoomed to failure. Lacking the essential business experience and the ability to coöperate, they were soon undone, and after a few years little more was heard of coöperation.

In the meantime another economic movement gained momentum under the leadership of George Henry Evans, who was a land reformer and may be called a precursor of Henry George. Evans inaugurated a campaign for free farms to entice to the land the unprosperous toilers of the city. In spite of the vast areas of the public domain still unoccupied, the cities were growing denser and larger and filthier by reason of the multitudes from Ireland and other countries who preferred to cast themselves into the eager maw of factory towns rather than go out as agrarian pioneers. To such Evans and other agrarian reformers made their appeal. For example, a handbill distributed everywhere in 1846 asked:

Are you an American citizen? Then you are a joint-owner of the public lands. Why not take enough of your property to provide yourself a home? Why not vote yourself a farm?

Are you a party follower? Then you have long enough employed your vote to benefit scheming office seekers. Use it for once to benefit yourself: Vote yourself a farm.

Are you tired of slavery — of drudging for others — of poverty and its attendant miseries? Then, vote yourself a farm.

Would you free your country and the sons of toil everywhere from the heartless, irresponsible mastery of the aristocracy of avarice? . . . Then join with your neighbors to form a true American party . . . whose chief measures will be first to limit the quantity of land that any one may henceforth monopolize or inherit: and second to make the public lands free to actual settlers only, each having the right to sell his improvements to any man not possessed of other lands.

"Vote yourself a farm" became a popular shibboleth and a part of the standard programme of organized labor. The donation of public lands to heads of families, on condition of occupancy and cultivation for a term of years, was proposed in bills repeatedly introduced in Congress. But the cry of opposition went up from the older States that they would be bled for the sake of the newer, that giving land to the landless was encouraging idleness and wantonness and spreading demoralization, and that Congress had no more power to give away land than it had to give away money. These arguments had their effect at the Capitol, and it was not until the new Republican party came into power pledged to "a complete and satisfactory homestead measure" that the Homestead Act of 1862 was placed on the statute books.

A characteristic manifestation of the humanitarian impulse of the forties was the support given to labor in its renewed demand for a ten-hour day. It has already been indicated how this movement started in the thirties, how its object was achieved by a few highly organized trades, and how it was interrupted in its progress by the panic of

1837. The agitation, however, to make the ten-hour day customary throughout the country was not long in coming back to life. In March, 1840, an executive order of President Van Buren declaring ten hours to be the working day for laborers and mechanics in government employ forced the issue upon private employers. The earliest concerted action, it would seem, arose in New England, where the New England Workingmen's Association, later called the Labor Reform League, carried on the crusade. In 1845 a committee appointed by the Massachusetts Legislature to investigate labor conditions affords the first instance on record of an American legislature concerning itself with the affairs of the labor world to the extent of ordering an official investigation. The committee examined a number of factory operatives, both men and women, visited a few of the mills, gathered some statistics, and made certain neutral and specious suggestions. They believed the remedy for such evils as they discovered lay not in legislation but "in the progressive improvement in art and science, in a higher appreciation of man's destiny, in a less love for money, and a more ardent love for social happiness and intellectual superiority."

The first ten-hour law was passed in 1847 by the New Hampshire Legislature. It provided that "ten hours of actual labor shall be taken to be a day's work, unless otherwise agreed to by the parties," and that no minor under fifteen years of age should be employed more than ten hours a day without the consent of parent or guardian. This was the unassuming beginning of a movement to have the hours of toil fixed by society rather than by contract. This law of New Hampshire, which was destined to have a widespread influence, was hailed by the workmen everywhere with delight; mass meetings and processions proclaimed it as a great victory; and only the conservatives prophesied the worthlessness of such legislation. Horace Greeley sympathetically dissected the bill. He had little faith, it is true, in legislative interference with private contracts. "But," he asks, "who can seriously doubt that it is the duty of the Commonwealth to see that the tender frames of its youth are not shattered by excessively protracted toil? . . . Will any one pretend that ten hours per day, especially at confining and monotonous avocations which tax at once the brain and the sinews are not quite enough for any child to labor statedly and steadily?" The consent of guardian or parent he thought a fraud against the child that could be averted only by the positive command of the State specifically limiting the hours of child labor.

In the following year Pennsylvania enacted a law declaring ten hours a legal day in certain industries and forbidding children under twelve from working in cotton, woolen, silk, or flax mills. Children over fourteen, however, could, by special arrangement with parents or guardians, be compelled to work more than ten hours a day. "This act is very much of a humbug," commented Greeley, "but it will serve a good end. Those whom it was intended to put asleep will come back again before long, and, like Oliver Twist, 'want some more.'"

The ten-hour movement had thus achieved social recognition. It had the stanch support of such men as Wendell Phillips, Edward Everett, Horace Greeley, and other distinguished publicists and philanthropists. Public opinion was becoming so strong that both the Whigs and Democrats in their party platforms declared themselves in favor of the ten-hour day. When, in the summer of 1847, the British Parliament passed a ten-hour law, American unions sent congratulatory messages to the British workmen. Gradually the various States followed the example of New Hampshire and Pennsylvania — New Jersey in 1851, Ohio in 1852, and Rhode Island in 1853 — and the "ten-hour system" was legally established.

But it was one thing to write a statute and another to enforce it. American laws were, after all, based upon the ancient Anglo-Saxon principle of private contract. A man could agree to work for as many hours as he chose, and each employer could drive his own bargain. The cotton mill owners of Allegheny City, for example, declared that they would be compelled to run their mills twelve hours a day. They would not, of course, employ children under twelve, although they felt deeply concerned for the widows who would thereby lose the wages of their children. But they must run on a twelve-hour schedule to meet competition from other States. So they attempted to make special contracts with each employee. The workmen objected to this and struck. Finally they compromised on a ten-hour day and a sixteen per cent reduction in wages. Such an arrangement became a common occurrence in the industrial world of the middle of the century.

In the meantime the factory system was rapidly

recruiting women workers, especially in the New England textile mills. Indeed, as early as 1825 "tailoresses" of New York and other cities had formed protective societies. In 1829 the mill girls of Dover, New Hampshire, caused a sensation by striking. Several hundred of them paraded the streets and, according to accounts, "fired off a lot of gunpowder." In 1836 the women workers in the Lowell factories struck for higher wages and later organized a Factory Girls' Association which included more than 2,500 members. It was aimed against the strict regimen of the boarding houses, which were owned and managed by the mills. "As our fathers resisted unto blood the lordly avarice of the British Ministry," cried the strikers, "so we, their daughters, never will wear the yoke which has been prepared for us."

In this vibrant atmosphere was born the powerful woman's labor union, the Female Labor Reform Association, later called the Lowell Female Industrial Reform and Mutual Aid Society. Lowell became the center of a far-reaching propaganda characterized by energy and a definite conception of what was wanted. The women joined in strikes, carried banners, sent delegates to the labor conventions, and were zealous in propaganda. It was

the women workers of Massachusetts who first
forced the legislature to investigate labor conditions and who aroused public sentiment to a pitch
that finally compelled the enactment of laws for
the bettering of their conditions. When the mill
owners in Massachusetts demanded in 1846 that
their weavers tend four looms instead of three, the
women promptly resolved that "we will not tend
a fourth loom unless we receive the same pay per
piece as on three. . . . This we most solemnly
pledge ourselves to obtain."

In New York, in 1845, the Female Industry
Association was organized at a large meeting
held in the court house. It included "tailoresses,
plain and coarse sewing, shirt makers, book-fold-
ers and stickers, capmakers, straw-workers, dress-
makers, crimpers, fringe and lacemakers," and
other trades open to women "who were like op-
pressed." The New York *Herald* reported "about
700 females generally of the most interesting
age and appearance" in attendance. The president of the meeting unfolded a pitiable condition of affairs. She mentioned several employers
by name who paid only from ten to eighteen cents
a day, and she stated that, after acquiring skill
in some of the trades and by working twelve

to fourteen hours a day, a woman might earn twenty-five cents a day! "How is it possible," she exclaimed, "that at such an income we can support ourselves decently and honestly?"

So we come to the fifties, when the rapid rise in the cost of living due to the influx of gold from the newly discovered California mines created new economic conditions. By 1853, the cost of living had risen so high that the length of the working day was quite forgotten because of the utter inadequacy of the wage to meet the new altitude of prices. Hotels issued statements that they were compelled to raise their rates for board from a dollar and a half to two dollars a day. Newspapers raised their advertising rates. Drinks went up from six cents to ten and twelve and a half cents. In Baltimore, the men in the Baltimore and Ohio Railway shops struck. They were followed by all the conductors, brakemen, and locomotive engineers. Machinists employed in other shops soon joined them, and the city's industries were virtually paralyzed. In New York nearly every industry was stopped by strikes. In Philadelphia, Boston, Pittsburgh, in cities large and small, the striking workmen made their demands known.

By this time thoughtful laborers had learned the

futility of programmes that attempted to reform
society. They had watched the birth and death
of many experiments. They had participated in
short-lived coöperative stores and shops; they had
listened to Owen's alluring words and had seen
his World Convention meet and adjourn; had witnessed national reform associations, leagues, and
industrial congresses issue their high-pitched resolutions; and had united on legislative candidates.
And yet the old world wagged on in the old way.
Wages and hours and working conditions could be
changed, they had learned, only by coercion. This
coercion could be applied, in general reforms, only
by society, by stress of public opinion. But in
concrete cases, in their own personal environment,
the coercion had to be first applied by themselves.
They had learned the lesson of letting the world
in general go its way while they attended to their
own business.

In the early fifties, then, a new species of union
appears. It discards lofty phraseology and the
attempt at world-reform and it becomes simply a
trade union. It restricts its house-cleaning to its
own shop, limits its demands to its trade, asks
for a minimum wage and minimum hours, and lays
out with considerable detail the conditions under

which its members will work. The weapons in its arsenal are not new — the strike and the boycott. Now that he has learned to distinguish essentials, the new trade unionist can bargain with his employer, and as a result trade agreements stipulating hours, wages, and conditions, take the place of the desultory and ineffective settlements which had hitherto issued from labor disputes. But it was not without foreboding that this development was witnessed by the adherents of the *status quo*. According to a magazine writer of 1853:

After prescribing the rate of remuneration many of the Trades' Unions go to enact laws for the government of the respective departments, to all of which the employer must assent. . . . The result even thus far is that there is found no limit to this species of encroachment. If workmen may dictate the hours and mode of service, and the number and description of hands to be employed, they may also regulate other items of the business with which their labor is connected. Thus we find that within a few days, in the city of New York, the longshoremen have taken by force from their several stations the horses and labor-saving gear used for delivering cargoes, it being part of their regulations not to allow of such competition.

The gravitation towards common action was felt over a wide area during this period. Some trades met in national convention to lay down

rules for their craft.   One of the earliest national
meetings was that of the carpet-weavers (1846) in
New York City, when thirty-four delegates, representing over a thousand operatives, adopted rules
and took steps to prevent a reduction in wages.
The National Convention of Journeymen Printers
met in 1850, and out of this emerged two years
later an organization called the National Typographical Union, which ten years later still, on
the admission of some Canadian unions, became
the International Typographical Union of North
America; and as such it flourishes today.   In 1855
the Journeymen Stone Cutters' Association of
North America was organized and in the following
year the National Trade Association of Hat Finish-
ers, the forerunner of the United Hatters of North
America.   In 1859 the Iron Molders' Union of
North America began its aggressive career.

The conception of a national trade unity was
now well formed; compactly organized national
and local trade unions with very definite industrial
aims were soon to take the place of ephemeral,
loose-jointed associations with vast and vague
ambitions.   Early in this period a new impetus
was given to organized labor by the historic decision of Chief Justice Shaw of Massachusetts in

a case[1] brought against seven bootmakers charged with conspiracy. Their offense consisted in attempting to induce all the workmen of a given shop to join the union and compel the master to employ only union men. The trial court found them guilty; but the Chief Justice decided that he did not "perceive that it is criminal for men to agree together to exercise their own acknowledged rights in such a manner as best to subserve their own interests." In order to show criminal conspiracy, therefore, on the part of a labor union, it was necessary to prove that either the intent or the method was criminal, for it was not a criminal offense to combine for the purpose of raising wages or bettering conditions or seeking to have all laborers join the union. The liberalizing influence of this decision upon labor law can hardly be over-estimated.

The period closed amidst general disturbances and forebodings, political and economic. In 1857 occurred a panic which thrust the problem of unemployment, on a vast scale, before the American consciousness. Instead of demanding higher wages, multitudes now cried for work. The marching masses, in New York, carried banners asking

[1] Commonwealth *vs.* Hunt.

for bread, while soldiers from Governor's Island and marines from the Navy Yard guarded the Custom House and the Sub-Treasury. From Philadelphia to New Orleans, from Boston to Chicago, came the same story of banks failing, railroads in bankruptcy, factories closing, idle and hungry throngs moving restlessly through the streets. In New York 40,000, in Lawrence 3500, in Philadelphia 20,000, were estimated to be out of work. Labor learned anew that its prosperity was inalienably identified with the well-being of industry and commerce; and society learned that hunger and idleness are the golden opportunity of the demagogue and agitator. The word "socialism" now appears more and more frequently in the daily press and always a synonym of destruction or of something to be feared. No sooner had business revived than the great shadow of internal strife was cast over the land, and for the duration of the Civil War the peril of the nation absorbed all the energies of the people.

CHAPTER IV

AMALGAMATION

After Appomattox, every one seemed bent on finding a short cut to opulence. To foreign observers, the United States was then simply a scrambling mass of selfish units, for there seemed to be among the American people no disinterested group to balance accounts between the competing elements — no leisure class, living on secured incomes, mellowed by generations of travel, education, and reflection; no bureaucracy arbitrarily guiding the details of governmental routine; no aristocracy, born umpires of the doings of their underlings. All the manifold currents of life seemed swallowed up in the commercial maelstrom. By the standards of what happened in this season of exuberance and intense materialism, the American people were hastily judged by critics who failed to see that the period was but the prelude to a maturer national life.

It was a period of a remarkable industrial expansion. Then "plant" became a new word in the phraseology of the market place, denoting the enlarged factory or mill and suggesting the hardy perennial, each succeeding year putting forth new shoots from its side. The products of this seedtime are seen in the colossal industrial growths of today. Then it was that short railway lines began to be welded into "systems," that the railway builders began to strike out into the prairies and mountains of the West, and that partnerships began to be merged into corporations and corporations into trusts, ever reaching out for the greater markets. Meanwhile the inventive genius of America was responding to the call of the time. In 1877 Bell telephoned from Boston to Salem; two years later, Brush lighted by electricity the streets of San Francisco. In 1882 Edison was making incandescent electric lights for New York and operating his first electric car in Menlo Park, New Jersey.

All these developments created a new demand for capital. Where formerly a manufacturer had made products to order or for a small number of known customers, now he made on speculation, for a great number of unknown customers, taking his risks in distant markets. Where formerly the banker had lent money on local security, now he gave credit to vast enterprises far away. New inventions or industrial processes brought on new speculations. This new demand for capital made necessary a new system of credits, which was erected at first, as the recurring panics disclosed, on sand, but gradually, through costly experience, on a more stable foundation.

The economic and industrial development of the time demanded not only new money and credit but new men. A new type of executive was wanted, and he soon appeared to satisfy the need. Neither a capitalist nor a merchant, he combined in some degree the functions of both, added to them the greater function of industrial manager, and received from great business concerns a high premium for his talent and foresight. This Captain of Industry, as he has been called, is the foremost figure of the period, the hero of the industrial drama.

But much of what is admirable in that generation of nation builders is obscured by the industrial anarchy which prevailed. Everybody was for himself — and the devil was busy harvesting the hindmost. There were "rate-wars," "cut-rate sales," secret intrigues, and rebates; and there were subterranean passages — some, indeed, scarcely under the surface — to council chambers, executive mansions, and Congress. There were extreme fluctuations of industry: prosperity was either at a very high level or depression at a very low one. Prosperity would bring on an expansion of credits, a rise in prices, higher cost of living, strikes and boycotts for higher wages; then depression would follow with the shutdown and that most distressing of social diseases, unemployment. During the panic of 1873–74 many thousands of men marched the streets crying earnestly for work.

Between the panics, strikes became a part of the economic routine of the country. They were expected, just as pay days and legal holidays are expected. Now for the first time came strikes that can only be characterized as stupendous. They were not mere slight economic disturbances; they were veritable industrial earthquakes. In 1873 the coal miners of Pennsylvania, resenting the truck system and the miserable housing which the mine owners forced upon them, struck by the tens of thousands. In Illinois, Indiana, Missouri, Maryland, Ohio, and New York strikes occurred in all sorts of industries. There were the usual parades and banners, some appealing, some insulting, and all the while the militia guarded property. In July, 1877, the men of the Baltimore and Ohio Railroad refused to submit to a fourth reduction in wages in seven years and struck. From Baltimore the resentment spread to Pennsylvania and culminated with riots in Pittsburgh. All the anthracite coal miners struck, followed by most of the bituminous miners of Ohio, Indiana, and Illinois. The militia were impotent to subdue the mobs; Federal troops had to be sent by President Hayes into many of the States; and a proclamation by the President commanded all citizens to keep the peace. Thus was Federal authority introduced to bolster up the administrative weakness of the States, and the first step was taken on the road to industrial nationalization.

The turmoil had hardly subsided when, in 1880, new strikes broke out. In the long catalogue of the strikers of that year are found the ribbon weavers of Philadelphia, Paterson, and New York, the stablemen of New York, New Jersey, and San Francisco, the cotton yard workers of New Orleans, the cotton weavers of New England and New York. the stockyard employees of Chicago and Omaha, the potters of Green Point, Long Island, the puddlers of Johnstown and Columbia, Pennsylvania, the machinists

of Buffalo, the tailors of New York, and the shoemakers of Indiana. The year 1882 was scarcely
less restive. But 1886 is marked in labor annals
as "the year of the great uprising," when twice
as many strikes as in any previous year were reported by the United States Commissioner of Labor, and when these strikes reached a tragic climax
in the Chicago Haymarket riots.

It was during this feverish epoch that organized
labor first entered the arena of national politics.
When the policy as to the national currency became an issue, the lure of cheap money drew labor
into an alliance in 1880 with the Greenbackers,
whose mad cry added to the general unrest. In
this, as in other fatuous pursuits, labor was only
responding to the forces and the spirit of the
hour. These have been called the years of amalgamation, but they were also the years of tumult,
for, while amalgamation was achieved, discipline
was not. Authority imposed from within was not
sufficient to overcome the decentralizing forces, and
just as big business had yet to learn by self-imposed
discipline how to overcome the extremely indi-
vidualistic tendencies which resulted in trade
anarchy, so labor had yet to learn through discipline the lessons of self-restraint. Moreover, in the

sudden expansion and great enterprises of these days, labor even more than capital lost in stability. One great steadying influence, the old personal relation between master and servant, which prevailed during the days of handicraft and even of the small factory, had disappeared almost completely. Now labor was put up on the market — a heartless term descriptive of a condition from which human beings might be expected to react violently — and they did, for human nature refused to be an inert, marketable thing.

The labor market must expand with the trader's market. In 1860 there were about one and a third million wage-earners in the United States; in 1870 well over two million; in 1880 nearly two and three-quarters million; and in 1890 over four and a quarter million. The city sucked them in from the country; but by far the larger augmentation came from Europe; and the immigrant, normally optimistic, often untaught, sometimes sullen and filled with a destructive resentment, and always accustomed to low standards of living, added to the armies of labor his vast and complex bulk.

There were two paramount issues — wages and the hours of labor — to which all other issues were and always have been secondary. Wages tend constantly to become inadequate when the standard of living is steadily rising, and they consequently require periodical readjustment. Hours of labor, of course, are not subject in the same degree to external conditions. But the tendency has always been toward a shorter day. In a previous chapter, the inception of the ten-hour movement was outlined. Presently there began the eight-hour movement. As early as 1842 the carpenters and caulkers of the Charleston Navy Yard achieved an eight-hour day; but 1863 may more properly be taken as the beginning of the movement. In this year societies were organized in Boston and its vicinity for the precise purpose of winning the eight-hour day, and soon afterwards a national Eight-Hour League was established with local leagues extending from New England to San Francisco and New Orleans.

This movement received an intelligible philosophy, and so a new vitality, from Ira Steward, a member of the Boston Machinists' and Blacksmiths' Union. Writing as a workingman for workingmen, Steward found in the standard of living the true reason for a shorter workday. With beautiful simplicity he pointed out to the laboring man that the shorter period of labor would not mean smaller pay, and to the employer that it would not mean a diminished output. On the contrary, it would be mutually beneficial, for the unwearied workman could produce as much in the shorter day as the wearied workman in the longer. "As long," Steward wrote, "as tired human hands do most of the world's hard work, the sentimental pretense of honoring and respecting the horny-handed toiler is as false and absurd as the idea that a solid foundation for a house can be made out of soap bubbles."

In 1865 Steward's pamphlet, *A Reduction of Hours and Increase of Wages*, was widely circulated by the Boston Labor Reform Association. It emphasized the value of leisure and its beneficial reflex effect upon both production and consumption. Gradually these well reasoned and conservatively expressed doctrines found champions such as Wendell Phillips, Henry Ward Beecher, and Horace Greeley to give them wider publicity and to impress them upon the public consciousness. In 1867 Illinois, Missouri, and New York passed eight-hour laws and Wisconsin declared eight hours a day's work for women and children. In 1868 Congress established an eight-hour day for public work. These were promising signs, though the battle was still far from being won. The eight-hour day has at last received "the sanction of society" — to use the words of President Wilson in his message to Congress in 1916, when he called for action to avert a great railway strike. But to win that sanction required over half a century of popular agitation, discussion, and economic and political evolution.

Such, in brief, were the general business conditions of the country and the issues which engaged the energies of labor reformers during the period following the Civil War. Meanwhile great changes were made in labor organizations. Many of the old unions were reorganized, and numerous local amalgamations took place. Most of the organizations now took the form of secret societies whose initiations were marked with naïve formalism and whose routines were directed by a group of officers with royal titles and fortified by signs, passwords, and ritual. Some of these orders decorated the faithful with high-sounding degrees. The societies adopted fantastic names such as "The Supreme Mechanical Order of the Sun," "The Knights of St. Crispin," and "The Noble Order of the Knights of Labor," of which more presently.

Meanwhile, too, there was a growing desire to unify the workers of the country by some sort of national organization. The outcome was a notable Labor Congress held at Baltimore in August, 1866, which included all kinds of labor organizations and was attended by seventy-seven delegates from thirteen States. In the light of subsequent events its resolutions now seem conservative and constructive. This Congress believed that, "all reforms in the labor movement can only be effected by an intelligent, systematic effort of the industrial classes . . . through the trades organizations." Of strikes it declared that "they have been injudicious and ill-advised, the result of impulse rather than principle, . . . and we would therefore discountenance them except as a *dernier ressort*, and when all means for an amicable and honorable adjustment has been abandoned." It issued a cautious and carefully phrased *Address to the Workmen throughout the Country*, urging them to organize and assuring them that "the first thing to be accomplished before we can hope for any great results is the thorough organization of all the departments of labor."

The National Labor Union which resulted from this convention held seven Annual Congresses,

and its proceedings show a statesmanlike conservatism and avoid extreme radicalism. This organization, which at its high tide represented a
membership of 640,000, in its brief existence was
influential in three important matters: first, it
pointed the way to national amalgamation and
was thus a forerunner of more lasting efforts in
this direction; secondly, it had a powerful influence
in the eight-hour movement; and, thirdly, it was
largely instrumental in establishing labor bureaus
and in gathering statistics for the scientific study
of labor questions.   But the National Labor Union
unfortunately went into politics; and politics
proved its undoing. Upon affiliating with the
Labor Reform party it dwindled rapidly, and after
1871 it disappeared entirely.

One of the typical organizations of the time
was the Order of the Knights of St. Crispin, so
named after the patron saint of the shoemakers,
and accessible only to members of that craft.   It
was first conceived in 1864 by Newell Daniels, a
shoemaker in Milford, Massachusetts, but no organization was effected until 1867, when the founder had moved to Milwaukee. The ritual and
constitution he had prepared was accepted then by
a group of seven shoemakers, and in four years

this insignificant mustard seed had grown into a
great tree. The story is told by Frank K. Foster,[1]
who says, speaking of the order in 1868: "It made
and unmade politicians; it established a monthly
journal; it started coöperative stores; it fought,
often successfully, against threatened reductions
of wages . . .; it became the undoubted foremost
trade organization of the world." But within five
years the order was rent by factionalism and in
1878 was acknowledged to be dead. It perished
from various causes — partly because it failed to
assimilate or imbue with its doctrines the thousands of workmen who subscribed to its rules
and ritual, partly because of the jealousy and
treachery which is the fruitage of sudden prosperity, partly because of failure to fulfill the fervent hopes of thousands who joined it as a prelude
to the industrial millennium; but especially it failed
to endure because it was founded on an economic
principle which could not be imposed upon society.
The rule which embraced this principle reads as
follows: "No member of this Order shall teach, or
aid in teaching, any fact or facts of boot or shoe-
making, unless the lodge shall give permission by

[1] *The Labor Movement, the Problem of Today*, edited by George
E. McNeill, Chapter VIII.

a three-fourths vote . . . provided that this article shall not be so construed as to prevent a father from teaching his own son. Provided also, that this article shall not be so construed as to hinder any member of this organization from learning any or all parts of the trade." The medieval craft guild could not so easily be revived in these days of rapid changes, when a new stitching machine replaced in a day a hundred workmen. And so the Knights of St. Crispin fell a victim to their own greed.

The Noble Order of the Knights of Labor, another of those societies of workingmen, was organized in November, 1869, by Uriah S. Stephens, a Philadelphia garment cutter, with the assistance of six fellow craftsmen. It has been said of Stephens that he was "a man of great force of character, a skilled mechanic, with the love of books which enabled him to pursue his studies during his apprenticeship, and feeling withal a strong affection for secret organizations, having been for many years connected with the Masonic Order." He was to have been educated for the ministry but, owing to financial reverses in his family, was obliged instead to learn a trade. Later he taught school for a few years, traveled extensively in the West Indies, South America, and California, and became an accomplished public speaker and a diligent observer of social conditions.

Stephens and his six associates had witnessed the dissolution of the local garment cutters' union. They resolved that the new society should not be limited by the lines of their own trade but should embrace "all branches of honorable toil." Subsequently a rule was adopted stipulating that at least three-fourths of the membership of lodges must be wage-earners eighteen years of age. Moreover, "no one who either sells or makes a living, or any part of it, by the sale of intoxicating drinks either as manufacturer, dealer, or agent, or through any member of his family, can be admitted to membership in this order; and no lawyer, banker, professional gambler, or stock broker can be admitted." They chose their motto from Solon, the wisest of lawgivers: "That is the most perfect government in which an injury to one is the concern of all"; and they took their preamble from Burke, the most philosophical of statesmen: "When bad men combine, the good must associate, else they will fall, one by one, an unpitied sacrifice in a contemptible struggle."

The order was a secret society and for years

kept its name from the public. It was generally known as the "Five Stars," because of the five asterisks that represented its name in all public notices. While mysterious initials and secret ceremonies gratified the members, they aroused a corresponding antagonism, even fear, among the public, especially as the order grew to giant size. What were the potencies of a secret organization that had only to post a few mysterious words and symbols to gather hundreds of workingmen in their halls? And what plottings went on behind those locked and guarded doors? To allay public hostility secrecy was gradually removed and in 1881 was entirely abolished — not, however, without serious opposition from the older members.

The atmosphere of high idealism in which the order had been conceived continued to be fostered by Stephens, its founder and its first Grand Master Workman. He extolled justice, discountenanced violence, and pleaded for "the mutual development and moral elevation of mankind." His exhortations were free from that narrow class antagonism which frequently characterizes the utterances of labor. One of his associates, too, invoked the spirit of chivalry, of true knighthood, when he said that the old trade union had failed because "it had failed to recognize the rights of man and looked only to the rights of tradesmen," that the labor movement needed "something that will develop more of charity, less of selfishness, more of generosity, less of stinginess and nearness, than the average society has yet disclosed to its members." Nor were these ideas and principles betrayed by Stephens's successor, Terence V. Powderly, who became Grand Master in 1879 and served during the years when the order attained its greatest power. Powderly, also, was a conservative idealist. His career may be regarded as a good example of the rise of many an American labor leader. He had been a poor boy. At thirteen he began work as a switchtender; at seventeen he was apprenticed as machinist; at nineteen he was active in a machinists' and blacksmiths' union. After working at his trade in various places, he at length settled in Scranton, Pennsylvania, and became one of the organizers of the Greenback Labor party. He was twice elected mayor of Scranton, and might have been elected for a third term had he not declined to serve, preferring to devote all his time to the society of which he was Grand Master. The obligations laid upon every member of the Knights of Labor were impressive:

Labor is noble and holy. To defend it from degradation; to divest it of the evils to body, mind and estate which ignorance and greed have imposed; to rescue the toiler from the grasp of the selfish — is a work worthy of the noblest and best of our race. In all the multifarious branches of trade capital has its combinations; and, whether intended or not, it crushes the manly hopes of labor and tramples poor humanity in the dust. We mean no conflict with legitimate enterprise, no antagonism to necessary capital; but men in their haste and greed, blinded by self-interests, overlook the interests of others and sometimes violate the rights of those they deem helpless. We mean to uphold the dignity of labor, to affirm the nobility of all who earn their bread by the sweat of their brows. We mean to create a healthy public opinion on the subject of labor (the only creator of values or capital) and the justice of its receiving a full, just share of the values or capital it has created. We shall, with all our strength, support laws made to harmonize the interests of labor and capital, for labor alone gives life and value to capital, and also those laws which tend to lighten the exhaustiveness of toil. To pause in his toil, to devote himself to his own interests, to gather a knowledge of the world's commerce, to unite, combine and coöperate in the great army of peace and industry, to nourish and cherish, build and develop the temple he lives in is the highest and noblest duty of man to himself, to his fellow men and to his Creator.

The phenomenal growth and collapse of the Knights of Labor is one of the outstanding events

in American economic history. The membership
in 1869 consisted of eleven tailors. This small
beginning grew into the famous Assembly No. 1.
Soon the ship carpenters wanted to join, and Assembly No. 2 was organized. The shawl-weavers
formed another assembly, the carpet-weavers another, and so on, until over twenty assemblies, cov-
ering almost every trade, had been organized in
Philadelphia alone. By 1875 there were eighty assemblies in the city and its vicinity. As the number of lodges multiplied, it became necessary to
establish a common agency or authority, and a
Committee on the Good of the Order was constituted to represent all the local units, but this committee was soon superseded by a delegate body
known as the District Assembly. As the movement spread from city to city and from State to
State, a General Assembly was created in 1878
to hold annual conventions and to be the supreme
authority of the order. In 1883 the membership of
the order was 52,000; within three years, it had
mounted to over 700,000; and at the climax of
its career the society boasted over 1,000,000 workmen in the United States and Canada who had
vowed fealty to its knighthood.

It is not to be imagined that every member

of this vast horde so suddenly brought together understood the obligations of the workman's chivalry. The selfish and the lawless rushed in with the prudent and sincere. But a resolution of the executive board to stop the initiation of new members came too late. The undesirable and radical element in many communities gained control of local assemblies, and the conservatism and intelligence of the national leaders became merely a shield for the rowdy and the ignorant who brought the entire order into popular disfavor.

The crisis came in 1886. In the early months of this turbulent year there were nearly five hundred labor disputes, most of them involving an advance in wages. An epidemic of strikes then spread over the country, many of them actually conducted by the Knights of Labor and all of them associated in the public mind with that order. One of the most important of these occurred on the Southwestern Railroad. In the preceding year, the Knights had increased their lodges in St. Louis from five to thirty, and these were under the domination of a coarse and ruthless district leader. When in February, 1886, a mechanic, working in the shops of the Texas and Pacific Railroad at Marshall, Texas, was discharged for cause and the road refused to reinstate him, a strike ensued which spread over the entire six thousand miles of the Gould system; and St. Louis became the center of the tumult. After nearly two months of violence, the outbreak ended in the complete collapse of the strikers. This result was doubly damaging to the Knights of Labor, for they had officially taken charge of the strike and were censured on the one hand for their conduct of the struggle and on the other for the defeat which they had sustained.

In the same year, against the earnest advice of the national leaders of the Knights of Labor, the employees of the Third Avenue Railway in New York began a strike which lasted many months and which was characterized by such violence that policemen were detailed to guard every car leaving the barns. In Chicago the freight handlers struck, and some 60,000 workmen stopped work in sympathy. On the 3d of May, at the McCormick Harvester Works, several strikers were wounded in a tussle with the police. On the following day a mass meeting held in Haymarket Square, Chicago, was harangued by a number of anarchists. When the police attempted to disperse the mob, guns were fired at the officers of the law and a bomb

was hurled into their throng, killing seven and
wounding sixty. For this crime seven anarchists
were indicted, found guilty, and sentenced to
be hanged. The Knights of Labor passed resolutions asking clemency for these murderers and
thereby grossly offended public opinion, and that
at a time when public opinion was frightened by
these outrages, angered by the disclosures of brazen plotting, and upset by the sudden consciousness that the immunity of the United States from
the red terror of Europe was at an end.

Powderly and the more conservative national
officers who were opposed to these radical machin-
ations were strong enough in the Grand Lodge in
the following year to suppress a vote of sympathy
for the condemned anarchists. The radicals thereupon seceded from the organization. This outcome, however, did not restore the order to the
confidence of the public, and its strength now rapidly declined. A loss of 300,000 members for the
year 1888 was reported. Early in the nineties,
financial troubles compelled the sale of the Philadelphia headquarters of the Knights of Labor and
the removal to more modest quarters in Washington. A remnant of members still retain an organization, but it is barely a shadow of the vast army of

Knights who at one time so hopefully carried on a crusade in every center of industry. It was not merely the excesses of the lawless but the multiplicity of strikes which alienated public sympathy. Powderly's repeated warnings that strikes, in and of themselves, were destructive of the stable position of labor were shown to be prophetic.

These excesses, however, were forcing upon the public the idea that it too had not only an interest but a right and a duty in labor disputes. Methods of arbitration and conciliation were now discussed in every legislature. In 1883 the House of Representatives established a standing committee on labor. In 1884 a national Bureau of Labor was created to gather statistical information. In 1886 President Cleveland sent to Congress a message which has become historic as the first presidential message devoted to labor. In this he proposed the creation of a board of labor commissioners who should act as official arbiters in labor disputes, but Congress was unwilling at that time to take so advanced a step. In 1888, however, it enacted a law providing for the settlement of railway labor disputes by arbitration, upon agreement of both parties.

Arbitration signifies a judicial attitude of mind, a

judgment based on facts. These facts are derived from specific conditions and do not grow out of broad generalizations. Arbitral tribunals are created to decide points in dispute, not philosophies of human action. The businesslike organization of the new trade union could as readily adapt itself to arbitration as it had already adapted itself, in isolated instances, to collective bargaining. A new stage had therefore been reached in the labor movement.

CHAPTER V

FEDERATION

EXPERIENCE and events had now paved the way for that vast centralization of industry which characterizes the business world of the present era. The terms sugar, coffee, steel, tobacco, oil, acquire on the stock exchange a new and precise meaning. Seventy-five per cent of steel, eighty-three per cent of petroleum, ninety per cent of sugar production are brought under the control of industrial combinations. Nearly one-fourth of the wage-earners of America are employed by great corportions. But while financiers are talking only in terms of millions, while super-organization is reaching its eager fingers into every industry, and while the units of business are becoming national in scope, the workingman himself is being taught at last to rely more and more upon group action in his endeavor to obtain better wages and working conditions. He is taught also to widen the area of his organization and to intensify its efforts. So, while the public reads in the daily and periodical press about the oil trust and the coffee trust, it is also being admonished against a labor trust and against two personages, both symbols of colossal economic unrest — the promoter, or the stalking horse of financial enterprise, and the walking delegate, or the labor union representative and only too frequently the advance agent of bitterness and revenge.

In response to the call of the hour there appeared the American Federation of Labor, frequently called in these later days the labor trust. The Federation was first suggested at Terre Haute, Indiana, on August 2, 1881, at a convention called by the Knights of Industry and the Amalgamated Labor Union, two secret societies patterned after the model common at that period. The Amalgamated Union was composed largely of disaffected Knights of Labor, and the avowed purpose of the Convention was to organize a new secret society to supplant the Knights. But the trades union element predominated and held up the British Trades Union and its powerful annual congress as a model. At this meeting the needs of intensive local organization, of trades autonomy, and of comprehensive team work were foreseen, and from the discussion there grew a plan for a second convention. With this meeting, which was held at Pittsburgh in November, 1881, the actual work of the new association began under the name, "The Federation of Organized Trades and Labor Unions of the United States of America and Canada."

When this Federation learned that a convention representing independent trade unions was called to meet in Columbus, Ohio, in December, 1886, it promptly altered its arrangements for its own annual session so that it, too, met at the same time and place. Thereupon the Federation effected a union with this independent body, which represented twenty-five organizations. The new organization was called the American Federation of Labor. Until 1889, this was considered as the first annual meeting of the new organization, but in that year the Federation resolved that its "continuity . . . be recognized and dated from the year 1881."

For some years the membership increased slowly; but in 1889 over 70,000 new members were reported, in 1900 over 200,000, and from that time the Federation has given evidence of such growth and prosperity that it easily is the most powerful labor organization America has known, and it takes its place by the side of the British Trades Union Congress as "the sovereign organization in the trade union world." In 1917 its membership reached 2,371,434, with 110 affiliated national unions, representing virtually every element of American industry excepting the railway brotherhoods and a dissenting group of electrical workers.

The foundation of this vast organization was the interest of particular trades rather than the interests of labor in general. Its membership is made up "of such Trade and Labor Unions as shall conform to its rules and regulations." The preamble of the Constitution states: "We therefore declare ourselves in favor of the formation of a thorough federation, embracing every trade and labor organization in America under the Trade Union System of organization." The Knights of Labor had endeavored to subordinate the parts to the whole; the American Federation is willing to bend the whole to the needs of the unit. It zealously sends out its organizers to form local unions and has made provision that "any seven wage workers of good character following any trade or calling" can establish a local union with federal affiliations.

This vast and potent organization is based upon

the principle of trade homogeneity — namely, that each trade is primarily interested in its own particular affairs but that all trades are interested in those general matters which affect all laboring men as a class. To combine effectually these dual interests, the Federation espouses the principle of home rule in purely local matters and of federal supervision in all general matters. It combines, with a great singleness of purpose, so diverse a variety of details that it touches the minutiæ of every trade and places at the disposal of the humblest craftsman or laborer the tremendous powers of its national influence. While highly centralized in organization, it is nevertheless democratic in operation, depending generally upon the referendum for its sanctions. It is flexible in its parts and can mobilize both its heavy artillery and its cavalry with equal readiness. It has from the first been managed with skill, energy, and great adroitness.

The supreme authority of the American Federation is its Annual Convention composed of delegates chosen from national and international unions, from state, central, and local trade unions, and from fraternal organizations. Experience has evolved a few simple rules by which the convention is safeguarded against political and factional debate and against the interruptions of "sore-heads." Besides attending to the necessary routine, the Convention elects the eleven national officers who form the executive council which guides the administrative details of the organization. The funds of the Federation are derived from a per capita tax on the membership. The official organ is the *American Federationist*. It is interesting to note in passing that over two hundred and forty labor periodicals together with a continual stream of circulars and pamphlets issue from the trades union press.

The Federation is divided into five departments, representing the most important groups of labor: the Building Trades, the Metal Trades, Mining, Railroad Employees, and the Union Label Trades. [1] Each of these departments has its own autonomous sphere of action, its own set of officers, its own financial arrangements, its own administrative details. Each holds an annual convention, in the same place and week, as the Federation. Each is made up of affiliated unions only and confines itself solely to the interest of its own trades. This sub-organization serves as an admirable clearing house

[1] There is in the Federation, however, a group of unions not affiliated with any of these departments.

and shock-absorber and succeeds in eliminating much of the friction which occurs between the several unions.

There are also forty-three state branches of the Federation, each with its own separate organization. There are annual state conventions whose membership, however, is not always restricted to unions affiliated with the American Federation. Some of these state organizations antedate the Federation.

There remain the local unions, into personal touch with which each member comes. There were in 1916 as many as 647 "city centrals," the term used to designate the affiliation of the unions of a city. The city centrals are smaller replicas of the state federations and are made up of delegates elected by the individual unions. They meet at stated intervals and freely discuss questions relating to the welfare of organized labor in general as well as to local labor conditions in every trade. Indeed, vigilance seems to be the watchword of the Central. Organization, wages, trade agreements, and the attitude of public officials and city councils which even remotely might affect labor rarely escape their scrutiny. This oldest of all the groups of labor organizations remains the most vital part of the Federation.

The success of the American Federation of Labor is due in large measure to the crafty generalship of its President, Samuel Gompers, one of the most astute labor leaders developed by American economic conditions. He helped organize the Federation, carefully nursed it through its tender years, and boldly and unhesitatingly used its great power in the days of its maturity. In fact, in a very real sense the Federation is Gompers, and Gompers is the Federation. Born in London of Dutch-Jewish lineage, on January 27, 1850, the son of a cigarmaker, Samuel Gompers was early apprenticed to that craft. At the age of thirteen he went to New York City, where in the following year he joined the first cigar-makers' union organized in that city. He enlisted all his boyish ardor in the cause of the trade union and, after he arrived at maturity, was elected successively secretary and president of his union. The local unions were, at that time, gingerly feeling their way towards state and national organization, and in these early attempts young Gompers was active. In 1887, he was one of the delegates to a national meeting which constituted the nucleus of what is now the Cigar-makers' International Union.

The local cigar-makers' union in which Gompers

received his necessary preliminary training was one
of the most enlightened and compactly organized
groups of American labor. It was one of the first
American Unions to adopt in an efficient manner
the British system of benefits in the case of sick-
ness, death, or unemployment. It is one of the few
American unions that persistently encourages skill
in its craft and intelligence in its membership. It
has been a pioneer in collective bargaining and in
arbitration. It has been conservatively and yet
enthusiastically led and has generally succeeded
in enlisting the respect and coöperation of employers. This union has been the kindergarten and
preparatory school of Samuel Gompers, who, during all the years of his wide activities as the head
of the Federation of Labor, has retained his membership in his old local and has acted as first
vice-president of the Cigar-makers' International.
These early experiences, precedents and enthusi-
asms Gompers carried with him into the Federation of Labor. He was one of the original group
of trade union representatives who organized the
Federation in 1881. In the following year he was
its President. Since 1885 he has, with the exception of a single year, been annually chosen as
President. During the first years the Federation

was very weak, and it was even doubtful if the organization could survive the bitter hostility of the powerful Knights of Labor. It could pay its President no salary and could barely meet his expense account.[1] Gompers played a large part in the complete reorganization of the Federation in 1886. He subsequently received a yearly salary of $1000 so that he could devote all of his time to the cause. From this year forward the growth of the Federation was steady and healthy. In the last decade it has been phenomenal. The earlier policy of caution has, however, not been discarded — for caution is the word that most aptly describes the methods of Gompers. From the first, he tested every step carefully, like a wary mountaineer, before he urged his organization to follow. From the beginning Gompers has followed three general lines of policy. First, he has built the imposing structure of his Federation upon the autonomy of the constituent unions. This is the secret of the united enthusiasm of the Federation. It is the Anglo-Saxon instinct for home rule applied to trade union politics. In the tentative years of its early struggles, the Federation could hope for survival only upon the suffrance of the trade union, and

[1] In one of the early years this was $13.

today, when the Federation has become powerful, its potencies rest upon the same foundation.

Secondly, Gompers has always advocated frugality in money matters. His Federation is powerful but not rich. Its demands upon the resources of the trade unions have always been moderate, and the salaries paid have been modest.[1] When the Federation erected a new building for its headquarters in Washington a few years ago, it symbolized in its architecture and equipment this modest yet adequate and substantial financial policy. American labor unions have not yet achieved the opulence, ambitions, and splendors of the guilds of the Middle Ages and do not yet direct their activities from splendid guild halls.

In the third place, Gompers has always insisted upon the democratic methods of debate and referendum in reaching important decisions. However arbitrary and intolerant his impulses may have been, and however dogmatic and narrow his conclusions in regard to the relation of labor to society and towards the employer (and his Dutch inheritance gives him great obstinacy), he has

---

[1] Before 1899 the annual income of the Federation was less than $25,000; in 1901 it reached the $100,000 mark: and since 1903 it has exceeded $200,000.

astutely refrained from too obviously bossing his own organization.

With this sagacity of leadership Gompers has combined a fearlessness that sometimes verges on brazenness. He has never hesitated to enter a contest when it seemed prudent to him to do so. He crossed swords with Theodore Roosevelt on more than one occasion and with President Eliot of Harvard in a historic newspaper controversy over trade union exclusiveness. He has not been daunted by conventions, commissions, courts, congresses, or public opinion. During the long term of his Federation presidency, which is unparalleled in labor history and alone is conclusive evidence of his executive skill, scarcely a year has passed without some dramatic incident to cast the searchlight of publicity upon him — a court decision, a congressional inquiry, a grand jury inquisition, a great strike, a nation-wide boycott, a debate with noted public men, a political maneuver, or a foreign pilgrimage. Whenever a constituent union in the Federation has been the object of attack, he has jumped into the fray and has rarely emerged humiliated from the encounter. This is the more surprising when one recalls that he possesses the limitations of the zealot and the dogmatism of the partisan.

One of the most important functions of Gompers has been that of national lobbyist for the Federation. He was one of the earliest champions of the eight-hour day and the Saturday half-holiday. He has energetically espoused Federal child labor legislation, the restriction of immigration, alien contract labor laws, and employers' liability laws. He advocated the creation of a Federal Department of Labor which has recently developed into a cabinet secretariat. His legal *bête noire*, however, was the Sherman Anti-Trust Law as applied to labor unions. For many years he fought vehemently for an amending act exempting the laboring class from the rigors of that famous statute. President Roosevelt with characteristic candor told a delegation of Federation officials who called on him to enlist his sympathy in their attempt, that he would enforce the law impartially against lawbreakers, rich and poor alike. Roosevelt recommended to Congress the passage of an amendment exempting "combinations existing for and engaged in the promotion of innocent and proper purposes." An exempting bill was passed by Congress but was vetoed by President Taft on the ground that it was class legislation. Finally, during President Wilson's administration, the Federation accomplished its purpose, first indirectly by a rider on an appropriation bill, then directly by the Clayton Act, which specifically declared labor combinations, instituted for the "purpose of mutual help and . . . not conducted for profit," not to be in restraint of trade. Both measures were signed by the President. Encouraged by their success, the Federation leaders have moved with a renewed energy against the other legal citadel of their antagonists, the use of the injunction in strike cases.

Gompers has thus been the political watchman of the labor interests. Nothing pertaining, even remotely, to labor conditions escapes the vigilance of his Washington office. During President Wilson's administration, Gompers's influence achieved a power second to none in the political field, owing partly to the political power of the labor vote which he ingeniously marshalled, partly to the natural inclination of the dominant political party, and partly to the strategic position of labor in the war industries.

The Great War put an unprecedented strain upon the American Federation of Labor. In every center of industry laborers of foreign birth early showed their racial sympathies, and under the stimuli of the intriguing German and Austrian ambassadors sinister plots for crippling munitions plants and the shipping industries were hatched everywhere. Moreover, workingmen became restive under the burden of increasing prices, and strikes for higher wages occurred almost daily.

At the beginning of the War, the officers of the Federation maintained a calm and neutral attitude which increased in vigilance as the strain upon American patience and credulity increased. As soon as the United States declared war, the whole energies of the officials of the Federation were cast into the national cause. In 1917, under the leadership of Gompers, and as a practical antidote to the I. W. W. and the foreign labor and pacifist organization known as The People's Council, there was organized The American Alliance for Labor and Democracy in order "to Americanize the labor movement." Its campaign at once became nation wide. Enthusiastic meetings were held in the great manufacturing centers, stimulated to enthusiasm by the incisive eloquence of Gompers. At the annual convention of the Federation held in Buffalo in November, 1917, full endorsement was given to the Alliance by a vote of 21,602 to 402. In its formal statement the Alliance declared: "It is our purpose to try, by educational methods, to bring about a more American spirit in the labor movement, so that what is now the clear expression of the vast majority may become the conviction of all.   Where we find ignorance, we shall educate.   Where we find something worse, we shall have to deal as the situation demands.   But we are going to leave no stone unturned to put a stop to anti-American activities among workers."   And in this patriotic effort the Alliance was successful.

This was the first great step taken by Gompers and the Federation.   The second was equally important.   With characteristic energy the organization put forward a programme for the readjustment of labor to war conditions.   "This is labor's war" declared the manifesto issued by the Federation.   "It must be won by labor, and every stage in the fighting and the final victory must be made to count for humanity."   These aims were embodied in constructive suggestions adopted by the Council of National Defense appointed by President Wilson.   This programme was in a large measure the work of Gompers, who was a member of the Council.   The following outline shows the comprehensive nature of the view which the laborer took of the relation between task and the War. The plan embraced:

1. Means for furnishing an adequate supply of labor to war industries.

This included: (a) A system of labor exchanges. (b) The training of workers. (c) Agencies for determining priorities in labor demands. (d) Agencies for the dilution of skilled labor.

2. Machinery for adjusting disputes between capital and labor, without stoppage of work.

3. Machinery for safeguarding conditions of labor, including industrial hygiene, safety appliances, etc.

4. Machinery for safeguarding conditions of living, including housing, etc.

5. Machinery for gathering data necessary for effective executive action.

6. Machinery for developing sound public sentiment and an exchange of information between the various departments of labor administration, the numerous industrial plants, and the public, so as to facilitate the carrying out of a national labor programme.

Having thus first laid the foundations of a national labor policy and having, in the second place, developed an effective means of Americanizing, as far as possible, the various labor groups, the Federation took another step. As a third essential element in uniting labor to help to win the war, it turned its attention to the inter-allied solidarity of workingmen. In the late summer and autumn of 1917, Gompers headed an American labor mission to Europe and visited England, Belgium, France, and Italy. His frequent public utterances in numerous cities received particular attention in the leading European newspapers and were eagerly read in the allied countries. The pacifist group of the British Labour Party did not relish his outspokenness on the necessity of completely defeating the Teutons before peace overtures could be made. On the other hand, some of the ultraconservative papers misconstrued his sentiments on the terms which should be exacted from the enemy when victory was assured. This misunderstanding led to an acrid international newspaper controversy, to which Gompers finally replied: "I uttered no sentence or word which by the wildest imagination could be interpreted as advocating the formula 'no annexations, and no indemnities.' On the contrary, I have declared, both in the United States and in conferences and public meetings while abroad, that the German forces must be driven back from the invaded territory before even peace terms could be discussed, that Alsace-Lorraine should be returned to France, that the 'Irredente' should be returned to Italy, and that the imperialistic militarist machine which has so outraged the conscience of the world must be made to feel the indignation and righteous wrath of all liberty and peace loving peoples." This mission had a deep effect in uniting the labor populations of the allied countries and especially in cheering the over-wrought workers of Britain and France, and it succeeded in laying the foundation for a more lasting international labor solidarity.

This considerable achievement was recognized when the Peace Conference at Paris formed a Commission on International Labor Legislation. Gompers was selected as one of the American representatives and was chosen chairman. While the Commission was busy with its tasks, an international labor conference was held at Berne. Gompers and his colleagues, however, refused to attend this conference. They gave as their reasons for this aloofness the facts that delegates from the Central powers, with whom the United States was still at war, were in attendance; that the meeting was held "for the purpose of arranging socialist procedure of an

international character"; and that the convention
was irregularly called, for it had been announced as
an inter-allied conference but had been surreptitious-
ly converted into an international pacifist gathering, conniving with German and Austrian socialists.

Probably the most far-reaching achievement of
Gompers is the by no means inconsiderable con-
tribution he has made to that portion of the treaty
of peace with Germany relating to the international organization of labor. This is an entirely
new departure in the history of labor, for it attempts to provide international machinery for
stabilizing conditions of labor in the various sig-
natory countries. On the ground that "the well-
being, physical and moral, of the industrial wage-
earners is of supreme international importance,"
the treaty lays down guiding principles to be followed by the various countries, subject to such
changes as variations in climate, customs, and
economic conditions dictate. These principles are
as follows: labor shall not be regarded merely as a
commodity or an article of commerce; employers
and employees shall have the right of forming
associations; a wage adequate to maintain a reasonable standard of living shall be paid; an eight-
hour day shall be adopted; a weekly day of rest

shall be allowed; child labor shall be abolished and provision shall be made for the education of youth; men and women shall receive equal pay for equal work; equitable treatment shall be accorded to all workers, including aliens resident in foreign lands; and an adequate system of inspection shall be provided in which women should take part.

While these international adjustments were taking place, the American Federation began to anticipate the problems of the inevitable national labor readjustment after the war. Through a committee appointed for that purpose, it prepared an ample programme of reconstruction in which the basic features are the greater participation of labor in shaping its environment, both in the factory and in the community, the development of coöperative enterprise, public ownership or regulation of public utilities, strict supervision of corporations, restriction of immigration, and the development of public education. The programme ends by declaring that "the trade union movement is unalterably and emphatically opposed . . . to a large standing army."

During the entire period of the war, both at home and abroad, Gompers fought the pacifist and the socialist elements in the labor movement. At the same time he was ever vigilant in pushing forward the claims of trade unionism and was always beforehand in constructive suggestions. His life has spanned the period of great industrial expansion in America. He has had the satisfaction of seeing his Federation grow under his leadership at first into a national and then into an international force. Gompers is an orthodox trade unionist of the British School. Bolshevism is to him a synonym for social ruin. He believes that capital and labor should coöperate but that capital should cease to be the predominant factor in the equation. In order to secure this balance he believes labor must unite and fight, and to this end he has devoted himself to the federation of American trade unions and to their battle. He has steadfastly refused political preferment and has declined many alluring offers to enter private business. In action he is an opportunist — a shrewd, calculating captain, whose knowledge of human frailties stands him in good stead, and whose personal acquaintance with hundreds of leaders of labor, of finance, and of politics, all over the country, has given him an unusual opportunity to use his influence for the advancement of the cause of labor in the turbulent field of economic warfare.

The American Federation of Labor has been forced by the increasing complexity of modern industrial life to recede somewhat from its early trade union isolation. This broadening point of view is shown first in the recognition of the man of no trade, the unskilled worker. For years the skilled trades monopolized the Federation and would not condescend to interest themselves in their humble brethren. The whole mechanism of the Federation in the earlier period revolved around the organization of the skilled laborers. In England the great dockers' strike of 1889 and in America the lurid flare of the I. W. W. activities forced the labor aristocrat to abandon his pharisaic attitude and to take an interest in the welfare of the unskilled. The future will test the stability of the Federation, for it is among the unskilled that radical and revolutionary movements find their first recruits.

A further change in the internal policy of the Federation is indicated by the present tendency towards amalgamating the various allied trades into one union. For instance, the United Brotherhood of Carpenters and the Amalgamated Wood Workers' Association, composed largely of furniture makers and machine wood workers, combined a few years ago and then proceeded to absorb the Wooden Box Makers, and the Wood Workers in the shipbuilding industry. The general secretary of the new amalgamation said that the organization looked "forward with pleasurable anticipations to the day when it can truly be said that all men of the wood-working craft on this continent hold allegiance to the United Brotherhood of Carpenters and Joiners of America." A similar unification has taken place in the lumbering industry. When the shingle weavers formed an international union some fifteen years ago, they limited the membership "to the men employed in skilled departments of the shingle trade." In 1912 the American Federation of Labor sanctioned a plan for including in one organization all the workers in the lumber industry, both skilled and unskilled. This is a far cry from the minute trade autocracy taught by the orthodox unionist thirty years ago.

Today the Federation of Labor is one of the most imposing organizations in the social system of America. It reaches the workers in every trade. Every contributor to the physical necessities of our materialistic civilization has felt the far-reaching influence of confederated power. A sense of its strength pervades the Federation. Like a healthy, self-conscious giant, it stalks apace among our national organizations. Through its cautious yet pronounced policy, through its seeking after definite results and excluding all economic vagaries, it bids fair to overcome the disputes that disturb it from within and the onslaughts of Socialism and of Bolshevism that threaten it from without.

CHAPTER VI

THE TRADE UNION

THE trade union[1] forms the foundation upon which the whole edifice of the American Federation of Labor is built. Like the Federation, each particular trade union has a tripartite structure: there is first the national body called the Union, the International, the General Union, or the Grand Lodge; there is secondly the district division or council, which is merely a convenient general union in miniature; and finally there is the local individual union, usually called "the local." Some unions, such as the United Mine Workers, have a fourth division or subdistrict, but this is not the general practice.

The sovereign authority of a trade union is its general convention, a delegate body meeting at stated times. Some unions meet annually, some

[1] The term "trade union" is used here in its popular sense, embracing labor, trade, and industrial unions, unless otherwise specified.

biennially, some triennially, and a few determine by referendum when the convention is to meet. Sometimes a long interval elapses: the granite cutters, for instance, held no convention between 1880 and 1912, and the cigar-makers, after a convention in 1896, did not meet for sixteen years. The initiative and referendum are, in some of the more compact unions, taking the place of the general convention, while the small executive council insures promptness of administrative action.

The convention elects the general officers. Of these the president is the most conspicuous, for he is the field marshal of the forces and fills a large place in the public eye when a great strike is called. It was in this capacity that John Mitchell rose to sudden eminence during the historic anthracite strike in 1902, and George W. Perkins of the cigar-makers' union achieved his remarkable hold upon the laboring people. As the duties of the president of a union have increased, it has become the custom to elect numerous vice-presidents to relieve him. Each of these has certain specific functions to perform, but all remain the president's aides. One, for instance, may be the financier, another the strike agent, another the organizer, another the agitator. With such a group of virtual specialists

around a chieftain, a union has the immense advantage of centralized command and of highly
organized leadership.   The tendency, especially
among the more conservative unions, is to reëlect
these officers year after year.   The president of
the Carpenters' Union held his office for twenty
years, and John Mitchell served the miners as
president ten years.   Under the immediate supervision of the president, an executive board composed of all the officers guides the destinies of the
union.   When this board is not occupied with the
relations of the men to their employers, it gives its
judicial consideration to the more delicate and
more difficult questions of inter-union comity and
of local differences.

The local union is the oldest labor organization,
and a few existing locals can trace their origin as
far back as the decade preceding the Civil War.
Many more antedate the organization of the Federation.   Not a few of these almost historic local
unions have refused to surrender their complete
independence by affiliating with those of recent
origin, but they have remained merely isolated independent locals with very little general influence.
The vast majority of local unions are members of
the national trades union and of the Federation.

The local union is the place where the laborer comes into direct personal contact with this powerful entity that has become such a factor in his daily life. Here he can satisfy that longing for the recognition of his point of view denied him in the great factory and here he can meet men of similar condition, on terms of equality, to discuss freely and without fear the topics that interest him most. There is an immense psychic potency in this intimate association of fellow workers, especially in some of the older unions which have accumulated a tradition.

It is in the local union that the real life of the labor organization must be nourished, and the statesmanship of the national leaders is directed to maintaining the greatest degree of local autonomy consistent with the interests of national homogeneity. The individual laborer thus finds himself a member of a group of his fellows with whom he is personally acquainted, who elect their own officers, to a large measure fix their own dues, transact their own routine business, discipline their own members, and whenever possible make their own terms of employment with their employers. The local unions are obliged to pay their tithe into the greater treasury, to make stated reports, to appoint a certain roster of committees, and in certain small matters to conform to the requirements of the national union. On the whole, however, they are independent little democracies confederated, with others of their kind, by means of district and national organizations.

The unions representing the different trades vary in structure and spirit. There is an immense difference between the temper of the tumultuous structural iron workers and the contemplative cigar-makers, who often hire one of their number to read to them while engaged in their work, the favorite authors being in many instances Ruskin and Carlyle. Some unions are more successful than others in collective bargaining. Martin Fox, the able leader of the iron moulders, signed one of the first trade agreements in America and fixed the tradition for his union; and the shoemakers, as well as most of the older unions are fairly well accustomed to collective bargaining. In matters of discipline, too, the unions vary. Printers and certain of the more skilled trades find it easier to enforce their regulations than do the longshoremen and unions composed of casual foreign laborers. In size also the unions of the different trades vary. In 1910 three had a membership of over 100,000 each. Of these the United Mine Workers reached a total of 370,800, probably the largest trades union in the world. The majority of the unions have a membership between 1000 and 10,000, the average for the entire number being 5000; but the membership fluctuates from year to year, according to the conditions of labor, and is usually larger in seasons of contest. Fluctuation in membership is most evident in the newer unions and in the unskilled trades. The various unions differ also in resources. In some, especially those composed largely of foreigners, the treasury is chronically empty; yet at the other extreme the mine workers distributed $1,890,000 in strike benefits in 1902 and had $750,-000 left when the board of arbitration sent the workers back into the mines.

The efforts of the unions to adjust themselves to the quickly changing conditions of modern industry are not always successful. Old trade lines are constantly shifting, creating the most perplexing problem of inter-union amity. Over two score jurisdictional controversies appear for settlement at each annual convention of the American Federation. The Association of Longshoremen and the Seamen's Union, for example, both claim jurisdiction over employees in marine warehouses. The cigar-makers and the stogie-makers have also long been at swords' points. Who shall have control over the coopers who work in breweries — the Brewery Workers or the Coopers' Union? Who shall adjust the machinery in elevators — the Machinists or Elevator Constructors? Is the operator of a linotype machine a typesetter? So plasterers and carpenters, blacksmiths and structural iron workers, printing pressmen and plate engravers, hod carriers and cement workers, are at loggerheads; the electrification of a railway creates a jurisdictional problem between the electrical railway employees and the locomotive engineers; and the marble workers and the plasterers quarrel as to the setting of imitation marble. These quarrels regarding the claims of rival unions reveal the weakness of the Federation as an arbitral body. There is no centralized authority to impose a standard or principle which could lead to the settlement of such disputes. Trade jealousy has overcome the suggestions of the peacemakers that either the nature of the tools used, or the nature of the operation, or the character of the establishment be taken as the basis of settlement.

When the Federation itself fails as a peacemaker, it cannot be expected that locals will escape these controversies. There are many examples, often ludicrous, of petty jealousies and trade rivalries. The man who tried to build a brick house, employing union bricklayers to lay the brick and union painters to paint the brick walls, found to his loss that such painting was considered a bricklayer's job by the bricklayers' union, who charged a higher wage than the painters would have done. It would have relieved him to have the two unions amalgamate. And this in general has become a real way out of the difficulty. For instance, a dispute between the Steam and Hot Water Fitters and the Plumbers was settled by an amalgamation called the United Association of Journeymen Plumbers, Gas Fitters, Steam Fitters, and Steam Fitters' Helpers, which is now affiliated with the Federation. But the International Association of Steam, Hot Water, and Power Pipe Fitters and Helpers is not affiliated, and inter-union war results. The older unions, however, have a stabilizing influence upon the newer, and a genuine conservatism such as characterizes the British unions is becoming more apparent as age solidifies custom and lends respect to by-laws and constitutions. But even time cannot obviate the seismic effects of new inventions, and shifts in jurisdictional matters are always imminent. The dominant policy of the trade union is to keep its feet on the earth, no matter where its head may be, to take one step at a time, and not to trouble about the future of society. This purpose, which has from the first been the prompter of union activity, was clearly enunciated in the testimony of Adolph Strasser, a converted socialist, one of the leading trade union-ists, and president of the Cigar-makers' Union, before a Senate Committee in 1883:

Chairman: You are seeking to improve home matters first?

Witness: Yes sir, I lo k first to the trade I represent: I look first to cigars, to the interests of men who employ me to represent their interests.

Chairman: I was only asking you in regard to your ultimate ends.

Witness: We have no ultimate ends. We are going on from day to day. We are fighting only for immediate objects — objects that can be realized in a few years.

Chairman: You want something better to eat and to wear, and better houses to live in?

Witness: Yes, we want to dress better and to live better, and become better citizens gener-ally.

Chairman: I see that you are a little sensitive lest it should be thought that you are a mere theorizer. I do not look upon you in that light at all.

Witness: Well, we say in our constitution that we are opposed to theorists, and I have to represent the organization here. We are all practical men.

This remains substantially the trade union platform today. Trade unionists all aim to be "practical men."

The trade union has been the training school for the labor leader, that comparatively new and increasingly important personage who is a product of modern industrial society. Possessed of natural aptitudes, he usually passes by a process of logical evolution, through the important committees and offices of his local into the wider sphere of the national union, where as president or secretary, he assumes the leadership of his group. Circumstances and conditions impose a heavy burden upon him, and his tasks call for a variety of gifts. Because some particular leader lacked tact or a sense of justice or some similar quality, many a labor maneuver has failed, and many a labor organization has suffered in the public esteem. No other class relies so much upon wise leadership as does the laboring class. The average wage-earner is without experience in confronting a new situation or trained and superior minds. From his tasks he has learned only the routine of his craft. When he is faced with the necessity of prompt action, he is therefore obliged to depend upon his chosen captains for results.

In America these leaders have risen from the rank and file of labor. Their education is limited. The great majority have only a primary schooling. Many have supplemented this meager stock of learning by rather wide but desultory reading and by keen observation. A few have read law, and some have attended night schools. But all have graduated from the University of Life. Many of them have passed through the bitterest poverty, and all have been raised among toilers and from infancy have learned to sympathize with the toiler's point of view.[1] They are therefore by training and origin distinctly leaders of a class, with the outlook

[1] A well-known labor leader once said to the writer: " No matter how much you go around among laboring people, you will never really understand us unless you were brought up among us. There is a real gulf between your way of looking on life and ours. You can be only an investigator or an intellectual sympathizer with my people. But you cannot really understand our view point." Whatever of misconception there may be in this attitude, it nevertheless marks the actual temper of the average wage earner, in spite of the fact that in America many employers have risen from the ranks of labor.

upon life, the prejudices, the limitations, and the fervent hopes of that class.

In a very real sense the American labor leader is the counterpart of the American business man — intensively trained, averse to vagaries, knowing thoroughly one thing and only one thing, and caring very little for anything else.

This comparative restriction of outlook marks a sharp distinction between American and British labor leaders. In Britain such leadership is a distinct career for which a young man prepares himself. He is usually fairly well educated, for not frequently he started out to study for the law or the ministry and was sidetracked by hard necessity. A few have come into the field from journalism. As a result, the British labor leader has a certain veneer of learning and puts on a more impressive front than the American. For example, Britain has produced Ramsey MacDonald, who writes books and makes speeches with a rare grace: John Burns, who quotes Shakespeare or recites history with wonderful fluency: Keir Hardie, a miner from the ranks, who was possessed of a charming poetic fancy: Philip Snowden, who displays the spiritual qualities of a seer; and John Henderson, who combines philosophical power with skill in dialectics.

On the other hand, the rank and file of American labor is more intelligent and alert than that of British labor, and the American labor leader possesses a greater capacity for intensive growth and is perhaps a better specialist at rough and tumble fighting and bargaining than his British colleague. [1]

In a very real sense every trade union is typified by some aggressive personality. The Granite Cutters' National Union was brought into active being in 1877 largely through the instrumentality of James Duncan, a rugged fighter who, having federated the locals, set out to establish an eight-hour day through collective bargaining and to settle disputes by arbitration. He succeeded in forming a well-disciplined force out of the members of his craft, and even the employers did not escape the touch of his rod.

The Glassblowers' Union was saved from disruption by Dennis Hayes, who, as president of the national union, reorganized the entire force in the years 1896–99, unionized a dozen of the largest

[1] The writer recalls spending a day in one of the Midland manufacturing towns with the secretary of a local coöperative society a man who was steeped in Bergson's philosophy and talked of local botany and geology as fluently as on local labor conditions It would be difficult to duplicate this experience in America.

glass producing plants in the United States and succeeded in raising the wages fifteen per cent. He introduced methods of arbitration and collective agreements and established a successful system of insurance.

James O'Connell, the president of the International Association of Machinists, led his organization safely through the panic of 1893, reorganized it upon a broader basis, and introduced sick benefits. In 1901 after a long and wearisome dickering with the National Metal Trades Association, a shorter day was agreed upon, but, as the employers would not agree to a ten-hour wage for a nine-hour day, O'Connell led his men out on a general strike and won.

Thomas Kidd, secretary of the Wood-Workers' International Union, was largely responsible for the agreement made with the manufacturers in 1897 for the establishment of a minimum wage of fifteen cents an hour for a ten-hour day, a considerable advance over the average wage paid up to that time. Kidd was the object of severe attacks in various localities, and in Oshkosh, Wisconsin, where labor riots took place for the enforcement of the Union demands, he was arrested for conspiracy but acquitted by the trial jury.

When the Amalgamated Association of Iron and Steel Workers lost their strike at Homestead, Pennsylvania, in 1892, the union was thought to be dead. It was quietly regalvanized into activity, however, by Theodore Schaffer, who has displayed adroitness in managing its affairs in the face of tremendous opposition from the great steel manufacturers who refuse to permit their shops to be unionized.

The International Typographical Union, composed of an unusually intelligent body of men, owes its singular success in collective contracting largely to James M. Lynch, its national president. The great newspapers did not give in to the demands of the union without a series of struggles in which Lynch manipulated his forces with skill and tact. Today this is one of the most powerful unions in the country.

Entirely different was the material out of which D. J. Keefe formed his Union of Longshoremen, Marine and Transport Workers. His was a mass of unskilled workers, composed of many nationalities, accustomed to rough conditions, and not easily led. Keefe, as president of their International Union, has had more difficulty in restraining his men and in teaching them the obligations of a contract than

any other leader. At least on one occasion he
employed non-union men to carry out the agreement which his recalcitrant following had made
and broken.

The evolution of an American labor leader is
shown at its best in the career of John Mitchell,
easily the most influential trade unionist of this
generation. He was born on February 4, 1870, on
an Illinois farm, but at two years of age he lost his
mother and at four his father. With other lads of
his neighborhood he shared the meager privileges
of the school terms that did not interfere with
farm work. At thirteen he was in the coal mines in
Braidwood, Illinois, and at sixteen he was the out-
er doorkeeper in the local lodge of the Knights of
Labor. Eager to see the world, he now began a
period of wandering, working his way from State
to State. So he traversed the Far West and the
Southwest, alert in observing social conditions and
coming in contact with many types of men. These
wanderings stood him in lieu of an academic course,
and when he returned to the coal fields of Illinois
he was ready to settle down. From his Irish par-
entage he inherited a genial personality and a
gift of speech. These traits, combined with his
continual reading on economic and sociological

subjects, soon lifted him into local leadership. He became president of the village school board and of the local lodge of the Knights of Labor. He joined the United Mine Workers of America upon its organization in 1890. He rose rapidly in its ranks, was a delegate to the district and sub-district conventions, secretary-treasurer of the Illinois district, chairman of the Illinois legislative committee, member of the executive board, and national organizer. In January, 1898, he was elected national vice-president, and in the following autumn, upon the resignation of the president, he became acting president. The national convention in 1899 chose him as president, a position which he held for ten years. He has served as one of the vice-presidents of the American Federation of Labor since 1898, was for some years chairman of the Trade Agreement Department of the National Civic Federation and has held the position of Chairman of the New York State Industrial Commission.

When he rose to the leadership of the United Mine Workers, this union had only 43,000 members, confined almost exclusively to the bituminous regions of the West. [1] Within the decade of his

[1] Less than 10,000 out of 140,000 anthracite miners were members of the union.

presidency he brought virtually all the miners of the United States under his leadership. Wherever his union went, there followed sooner or later the eight-hour day, raises in wages of from thirteen to twenty-five per cent, periodical joint conventions with the operators for settling wage scales and other points in dispute, and a spirit of prosperity that theretofore was unknown among the miners.

In unionizing the anthracite miners, Mitchell had his historic fight with the group of powerful corporations that owned the mines and the railways which fed them. This great strike, one of the most significant in our history, attracted universal attention because of the issues involved, because a coal shortage threatened many Eastern cities, and because of the direct intervention of President Roosevelt. The central figure of this gigantic struggle was the miners' young leader, barely thirty years old, with the features of a scholar and the demeanor of an ascetic, marshaling his forces with the strategic skill of a veteran general.

At the beginning of the strike Mitchell, as president of the Union, announced that the miners were eager to submit all their grievances to an impartial arbitral tribunal and to abide by its decisions. The ruthless and prompt refusal of the mine owners to consider this proposal reacted powerfully in the strikers' favor among the public. As the long weeks of the struggle wore on, increasing daily in bitterness, multiplying the apprehension of the strikers and the restiveness of the coal consumers, Mitchell bore the increasing strain with his customary calmness and self-control.

After the parties had been deadlocked for many weeks, President Roosevelt called the mine owners and the union leaders to a conference in the White House. Of Mitchell's bearing, the President afterwards remarked: "There was only one man in the room who behaved like a gentleman, and that man was not I."

The Board of Arbitration eventually laid the blame on both sides but gave the miners the bulk of their demands. The public regarded the victory as a Mitchell victory, and the unions adored the leader who had won their first strike in a quarter of a century, and who had won universal confidence by his ability and demeanor in the midst of the most harassing tensions of a class war.[1]

[1] Mitchell was cross-examined for three days when he was testifying before the Anthracite Coal Strike Commission. Every weapon which craft, prejudice, and skill could marshal against him failed to ruffle his temper or to lead him into damaging admissions or contradictions.

John Mitchell's powerful hold upon public opinion today is not alone due to his superior intelligence, his self-possession, his business skill, nor his Irish gift of human accommodation, but to the greater facts that he was always aware of the grave responsibilities of leadership, that he realized the stern obligation of a business contract, and that he always followed the trade union policy of asking only for that which was attainable. Soon after the Anthracite strike he wrote:

I am opposed to strikes as I am opposed to war. As yet, however, the world with all its progress has not made war impossible: neither, I fear, considering the nature of men and their institutions, will the strike entirely disappear for years to come. . . .

This strike has taught both capital and labor that they owe certain obligations to society and that their obligations must be discharged in good faith. If both are fair and conciliatory, if both recognize the moral restraint of the state of society by which they are surrounded, there need be few strikes. They can, and it is better that they should, settle their differences between themselves. . . .

Since labor organizations are here, and here to stay, the managers of employing corporations must choose what they are to do with them. They may have the union as a present, active, and unrecognized force, possessing influence for good or evil, but without direct responsibility; or they may deal with it, give it responsibility as well as power, define and regulate that power, and make the union an auxiliary in the promotion of stability and discipline and the amicable adjustment of all local disputes.

CHAPTER VII

THE RAILWAY BROTHERHOODS

THE solidarity and statesmanship of the trade unions reached perfection in the railway "Brotherhoods." Of these the Brotherhood of Locomotive Engineers[1] is the oldest and most powerful. It grew out of the union of several early associations; one of these was the National Protective Association formed after the great Baltimore and Ohio strike in 1854; another was the Brotherhood of the Footboard, organized in Detroit after the bitter strike on the Michigan Central in 1862. Though born thus of industrial strife, this railroad union has nevertheless developed a poise and a conservatism which have been its greatest assets in the

---

[1] Up to this time the Brotherhoods have not affiliated with the Knights of Labor nor with the American Federation of Labor. After the passage of the eight-hour law by Congress in 1916, definite steps were taken towards affiliating the Railway Brotherhoods with the Federation, and at its annual convention in 1919 the Federation voted to grant them a charter.

numerous controversies engaging its energies. No other union has had a more continuous and hard-headed leadership, and no other has won more universal respect both from the public and from the employer.

This high position is largely due, no doubt, to the fact that the Brotherhood of Locomotive Engineers is composed of a very select and intelligent class of men. Every engineer must first serve an apprenticeship as a fireman, which usually lasts from four to twelve years. Very few are advanced to the rank of engineer in less than four years. The firemen themselves are selected men who must pass several physical examinations and then submit to the test of as arduous an apprenticeship as modern industrialism affords. In the course of an eight- to twelve-hour run firemen must shovel from fifteen to twenty-five tons of coal into the blazing fire box of a locomotive. In winter they are constantly subjected to hot blasts from the furnace and freezing drafts from the wind. Records show that out of every hundred who begin as firemen only seventeen become engineers and of these only six ever become passenger engineers. The mere strain on the eyes caused by looking into the coal blaze eliminates 17 per cent. Those who eventually become engineers are therefore a select group as far as physique is concerned.

The constant dangers accompanying their daily work require railroad engineers to be no less dependable from the moral point of view. The history of railroading is as replete with heroism as is the story of any war. A coward cannot long survive at the throttle. The process of natural selection which the daily labor of an engineer involves the Brotherhood has supplemented by most rigid moral tests. The character of every applicant for membership is thoroughly scrutinized and must be vouched for by three members. He must demonstrate his skill and prove his character by a year's probation before his application is finally voted upon. Once within the fold, the rules governing his conduct are inexorable. If he shuns his financial obligations or is guilty of a moral lapse, he is summarily expelled. In 1909, thirty-six members were expelled for "unbecoming conduct." Drunkards are particularly dangerous in railroading. When the order was only five years old and still struggling for its life, it nevertheless expelled 172 members for drunkenness. In proven cases of this sort the railway authorities are notified, the offending engineer is dismissed from the service, and the shame of these culprits is published to the world in the *Locomotive Engineers' Journal*, which reaches every member of the order. There is probably no other club or professional organization so exacting in its demands that its members be self-respecting, faithful, law-abiding, and capable; and surely no other is so summary and far-reaching in its punishments.

Today ninety per cent of all the locomotive engineers in the United States and Canada belong to this union. But the Brotherhood early learned the lesson of exclusion. In 1864 after very annoying experiences with firemen and other railway employees on the Pittsburgh, Fort Wayne and Chicago Railroad, it amended its constitution and excluded firemen and machinists from the order. This exclusive policy, however, is based upon the stern requirements of professional excellence and is not displayed towards engineers who are not members of the Brotherhood. Towards them there is displayed the greatest toleration and none of the narrow spirit of the "closed shop." The non-union engineer is not only tolerated but is even on occasion made the benefici ry of the activities of the union. He shares, for example, in the rise of wages and readjustment of runs. There are even cases on record where the railroad unions have taken up a specific grievance between a non-union man and his employer and have attempted a readjustment.

From the inception of the Brotherhood, the policy of the order towards the employing railroad company has been one of business and not of sentiment. The Brotherhood has held that the relation between the employer and employee concerning wages, hours, conditions of labor, and settlement of difficulties should be on the basis of a written contract; that the engineer as an individual was at a manifest disadvantage in making such a contract with a railway company; that he therefore had a right to join with his fellow engineers in pressing his demands and therefore had the right to a collective contract. Though for over a decade the railways fought stubbornly against this policy, in the end every important railroad of this country and Canada gave way. It is doubtful, indeed, if any of them would today be willing to go back to the old method of individual bargaining, for the Brotherhood has insisted upon the inviolability of a contract once entered into. It has consistently held that "a bargain is a bargain, even if it is a poor bargain." Members who violate an agreement are expelled, and any local lodge which is guilty of such an offense has its charter revoked.[1]

Once the practice of collective contract was fixed, it naturally followed that some mechanism for adjusting differences would be devised. The Brotherhood and the various roads now maintain a general board of adjustment for each railway system. The Brotherhood is strict in insisting that the action of this board is binding on all its members. This method of bargaining and of settling disputes has been so successful that since 1888 the Brotherhood has not engaged in an important strike. There have been minor disturbances, it is true, and several nation-wide threats, but no serious strikes inaugurated by the engineers. This great achievement of the Brotherhood could not have been possible without keen ability in the leaders and splendid solidarity among the men.

The individual is carefully looked after by the Brotherhood. The Locomotive Engineers' Mutual Life and Accident Insurance Association is an integral part of the Brotherhood, though it maintains a separate legal existence in order to comply

[1] In 1905 in New York City 393 members were expelled and their charter was revoked for violation of their contract of employment by taking part in a sympathetic strike of the subway and elevated roads.

with the statutory requirements of many States.[1]
Every member must carry an insurance policy in
this Association for not less than $1500, though
he cannot take more than $4500. The policy is car-
ried by the order if the engineer becomes sick or
is otherwise disabled, but if he fails to pay assess-
ments when he is in full health, he gives grounds
for expulsion. There is a pension roll of three hundred disabled engineers, each of whom receives $25
a month; and the four railroad brotherhoods together maintain a Home for Disabled Railroad
Men at Highland Park, Illinois.

The technical side of engine driving is emphasized by the *Locomotive Engineers' Journal*, which
goes to every member, and in discussions in the
stated meetings of the Brotherhood. Intellectual
and social interests are maintained also by lec-
ture courses, study clubs, and women's auxiliaries.
Attendance upon the lodge meetings has been
made compulsory with the intention of insuring
the order from falling prey to a designing minority

[1] The following figures show the status of the Insurance Association in 1918. The total amount of life insurance in force was
$161,205,500.00. The total amount of claims paid from 1868 to
1918 was $41,085,123.04. The claims paid in 1918 amounted to
$3,014,540.22. The total amount of indemnity insurance in force
in 1918 was $12,486,397.50. The total claims paid up to 1918
were $1,624,537.61; and during 1918, $241,780.08.

— a condition which has proved the cause of the downfall of more than one labor union.

The Brotherhood of Engineers is virtually a large and prosperous business concern. Its management has been enterprising and provident; its treasury is full; its insurance policies aggregate many millions; it owns a modern skyscraper in Cleveland which cost $1,250,000 and which yields a substantial revenue besides housing the Brotherhood offices.

The engineers have, indeed, succeeded in forming a real Brotherhood — a "feudal" brotherhood an opposing lawyer once called them — reëstablishing the medieval guild-paternalism so that each member is responsible for every other and all are responsible for each. They therefore merge themselves through self-discipline into a powerful unity for enforcing their demands and fulfilling their obligations.

The supreme authority of the Brotherhood is the Convention, which is composed of delegates from the local subdivisions. In the interim between conventions, the authorized leader of the organization is the Grand Chief Engineer, whose decrees are final unless reversed by the Convention. This authority places a heavy responsibility upon him, but the Brotherhood has been singularly fortunate in its choice of chiefs.   Since 1873 there have been only two.   The first of these was P. M. Arthur, a sturdy Scot, born in 1831 and brought to America in boyhood.   He learned the blacksmith and machinist trades but soon took to railroading, in which he rose rapidly from the humblest place to the position of engineer on the New York Central lines.   He became one of the charter members of the Brotherhood in 1863 and was active in its affairs from the first.   In 1873 the union became involved in a bitter dispute with the Pennsylvania Railroad, and Arthur, whose prompt and energetic action had already designated him as the natural leader of the Brotherhood, was elected to the chieftainship. For thirty years he maintained his prestige and became a national figure in the labor world.   He died suddenly at Winnipeg in 1903 while speaking at the dinner which closed the general convention of the Brotherhood.

When P. M. Arthur joined the engineers' union, the condition of locomotive engineers was unsatisfactory.   Wages were unstable; working conditions were hard and, in the freight service, intolerable. For the first decade of the existence of the Brotherhood, strike after strike took place in the effort to establish the right of organizing and the principle of the collective contract. Arthur became head of the order at the beginning of the period of great financial depression which followed the first Civil War boom and which for six years threatened wages in all trades. But Arthur succeeded, by shrewd and careful bargaining, in keeping the pay of engineers from slipping down and in some instances he even advanced them. Gradually strikes became more and more infrequent; and the railways learned to rely upon his integrity, and the engineers to respect his skill as a negotiator. He proved to the first that he was not a labor agitator and to the others that he was not a visionary.

Year by year, Arthur accumulated prestige and power for his union by practical methods and by being content with a step at a time. This success, however, cost him the enmity of virtually all the other trades unionists. To them the men of his order were aristocrats, and he was lord over the aristocrats. He is said to have "had rare skill in formulating reasonable demands, and by consistently putting moderate demands strongly instead of immoderate demands weakly he kept the good will of railroad managers, while steadily obtaining better terms for his men." In this practice, he could not succeed without the solid good will of the members of the Brotherhood; and this good will was possible only in an order which insisted upon that high standard of personal skill and integrity essential to a first-class engineer. Arthur possessed a genial, fatherly personality. His Scotch shrewdness was seen in his own real estate investments, which formed the foundation of an independent fortune. He lived in an imposing stone mansion in Cleveland; he was a director in a leading bank; and he identified himself with the public affairs of the city.

When Chief Arthur died, the Assistant Grand Chief Engineer, A. B. Youngson, who would otherwise have assumed the leadership for the unexpired term, was mortally ill and recommended the advisory board to telegraph Warren S. Stone an offer of the chieftainship. Thus events brought to the fore a man of marked executive talent who had hitherto been unknown but who was to play a tremendous rôle in later labor politics. Stone was little known east of the Mississippi. He had spent most of his life on the Rock Island system, had visited the East only once, and had attended but one meeting of the General Convention. In the West, however, he had a wide reputation for sound sense, and, as chairman of the general committee of adjustment of the Rock Island system, he had made a deep impression on his union and his employers. Born in Ainsworth, Iowa, in 1860, Stone had received a high school education and had begun his railroading career as fireman on the Rock Island when he was nineteen years old. At twenty-four he became an engineer. In this capacity he spent the following nineteen years on the Rock Island road and then accepted the chieftainship of the Brotherhood.

Stone followed the general policy of his predecessor, and brought to his tasks the energy of youth and the optimism of the West. When he assumed the leadership, the cost of living was rising rapidly and he addressed himself to the adjustment of wages. He divided the country into three sections in which conditions were similar. He began in the Western section, as he was most familiar with that field, and asked all the general managers of that section to meet the Brotherhood for a wage conference. The roads did not accept his invitation until it was reënforced by the threat of a Western strike. The conference was a memorable one. For nearly three weeks the grand officers of the Brotherhood wrangled and wrought with the managers of the Western roads, who yielded ground slowly, a few pennies' increase at a time, until a satisfactory wage scale was reached. Similarly the Southern section was conquered by the inexorable hard sense and perseverance of this new chieftain.

The dispute with the fifty-two leading roads in the so-called Eastern District, east of the Mississippi and north of the Norfolk and Western Railroad, came to a head in 1912. The engineers demanded that their wages should be "standardized" on a basis that one hundred miles or less, or ten hours or less, constitute a day's work; that is, the inequalities among the different roads should be leveled and similar service on the various roads be similarly rewarded. They also asked that their wages be made equal to the wages on the Western roads and presented several minor demands. All the roads concerned flatly refused to grant the demand for a standardized and increased wage, on the ground that it would involve an increased expenditure of $7,000,000 a year. This amount could be made up only by increased rates, which the Interstate Commerce Commission must sanction, or by decreased dividends, which would bring a real hardship to thousands of stockholders.

The unions were fully prepared for a strike which would paralyze the essential traffic supplying approximately 38,000,000 people. Through the agency of Judge Knapp of the United States Commerce Court and Dr. Neill of the United States Department of Labor, and under the authority of the Erdman Act, there was appointed a board of arbitration composed of men whose distinction commanded national attention. P. H. Morrissey, a former chief of the Conductors' and Trainmen's Union, was named by the engineers. President Daniel Willard of the Baltimore and Ohio Railroad, known for his fair treatment of his employees, was chosen by the roads. The Chief Justice of the United States Supreme Court, the Commissioner of Labor, and the presiding judge of the United States Commerce Court designated the following members of the tribunal: Oscar S. Straus, former Secretary of Commerce and Labor, chairman; Albert Shaw, editor of the *Review of Reviews;* Otto M. Eidlitz, former president of the Building Trades Association; Charles R. Van Hise, president of the University of Wisconsin; and Frederick N. Judson, of the St. Louis bar.

After five months of hearing testimony and deliberation, this distinguished board brought in a report that marked, it was hoped, a new epoch in railway labor disputes, for it recognized the rights of the public, the great third party to such disputes.

It granted the principle of standardization and minimum wage asked for by the engineers, but it allowed an increase in pay which was less by one-half than that demanded. In order to prevent similar discord in the future, the board recommended the establishment of Federal and state wage commissions with functions pertaining to wage disputes analogous to those of the public service commissions in regard to rates and capitalization. The report stated that, "while the railway employees feel that they cannot surrender their right to strike, if there were a wage commission which would secure them just wages the necessity would no longer exist for the exercise of their power. It is believed that, in the last analysis, the only solution — unless we are to rely solely upon the restraining power of public opinion — is to qualify the principle of free contract in the railroad service."[1]

While yielding to the wage findings of the board,

[1] The board recognized the great obstacles in the way of such a solution but went on to say: "The suggestion, however, grows out of a profound conviction that the food and clothing of our people, the industries and the general welfare of our nation, cannot be permitted to depend upon the policies and dictates of any particular group of men, whether employers or employees." And this conviction has grown apace with the years until it stands to-day as the most potent check to aggression by either trade unions or capital.

P. H. Morrissey vigorously dissented from the principle of the supremacy of public interest in these matters. He made clear his position in an able minority report: "I wish to emphasize my dissent from that recommendation of the board which in its effect virtually means compulsory arbitration for the railroads and their employees. Regardless of any probable constitutional prohibition which might operate against its being adopted, it is wholly impracticable. The progress towards the settlement of disputes between the railways and their employees without recourse to industrial warfare has been marked. There is nothing under present conditions to prevent its continuance. We will never be perfect, but even so, it will be immeasurably better than it will be under conditions such as the board proposes."

The significance of these words was brought out four years later when the united railway brotherhoods made their famous *coup* in Congress. For the time being, however, the public with its usual self-assurance thought the railway employee question was solved, though the findings were for one year only.[1]

[1] The award dated back to May 1, 1912, and was valid only one year from that date.

Daniel Willard speaking for the railroads, said: "My acceptance of the award as a whole does not signify my approval of all the findings in detail. It is intended, however, to indicate clearly that, although the award is not such as the railroads had hoped for, nor is it such as they felt would be justified by a full consideration of all the facts, yet having decided to submit this case to arbitration and having been given ample opportunity to present the facts and arguments in support of their position, they now accept without question the conclusion which was reached by the board appointed to pass upon the matter at issue."

A comparison of these statements shows how the balance of power had shifted, since the days when railway policies reigned supreme, from the corporation to the union. The change was amply demonstrated by the next grand entrance of the railway brotherhoods upon the public stage. After his victory in the Western territory, Chief Stone remarked: "Most labor troubles are the result of one of two things, misrepresentation or misunderstanding. Unfortunately, negotiations are sometimes entrusted to men who were never intended by nature for this mission, since they cannot discuss a question without losing their temper. . . .

It may be laid down as a fundamental **principle** without which no labor organization can hope to exist, that it must carry out its contracts. No employer can be expected to live up to a contract that is not regarded binding by the union."

The other railway brotherhoods to a considerable degree follow the model set by the engineers. The Order of Railway Conductors developed rapidly from the Conductors' Union which was organized by the conductors of the Illinois Central Railroad at Amboy, Illinois, in the spring of 1868. In the following July this union was extended to include all the lines in the State. In November of the same year a call to conductors on all the roads in the United States and the British Provinces was issued to meet at Columbus, Ohio, in December, to organize a general brotherhood. Ten years later the union adopted its present name. It has an ample insurance fund[1] based upon the principle that policies are not matured but members arriving at the age of seventy years are relieved from further payments. About thirty members are thus annually retired. At Cedar Rapids, Iowa, the national headquarters, the order publishes *The Railway*

[1] In 1919 the total amount of outstanding insurance was somewhat over $90,000,000.

Conductor, a journal which aims not only at the solidarity of the membership but at increasing their practical efficiency.

The conductors are a conservative and carefully selected group of men. Each must pass through a long term of apprenticeship and must possess ability and personality. The order has been carefully and skillfully led and in recent years has had but few differences with the railways which have not been amicably settled. Edgar E. Clark was chosen president in 1890 and served until 1906, when he became a member of the Interstate Commerce Commission. He was born in 1856, received a public school education, and studied for some time in an academy at Lima, New York. At the age of seventeen, he began railroading and served as conductor on the Northern Pacific and other Western lines. He held numerous subordinate positions in the Brotherhood and in 1889 became its vice-president. He was appointed by President Roosevelt as a member of the Anthracite Coal Strike Commission in 1902 and is generally recognized as one of the most judicial heads in the labor world. He was succeeded as president of the order by Austin B. Garretson, who was born in Winterset, Iowa, in 1856. He began his railroad career at nineteen years of age, became a conductor on the Burlington system, and had a varied experience on several Western lines, including the Mexican National and Mexican Central railways. His rise in the order was rapid and in 1889 he became vice-president. One of his intimate friends wrote that "in his capacity as Vice-President and President of the Order he has written more schedules and successfully negotiated more wage settlements, including the eight-hour day settlement in 1916, under the method of collective bargaining than any other labor leader on the American continent."

Garretson has long served as a member of the executive committee of the National Civic Federation and in 1912 was appointed by President Wilson a member of the Federal Commission on Industrial Relations. A man of great energy and force of character, he has recently assumed a leading place in labor union activities.

In addition to the locomotive engineers and the conductors, the firemen also have their union. Eleven firemen of the Erie Railroad organized a brotherhood at Port Jervis, New York, in December, 1873, but it was a fraternal order rather than a trade union. In 1877, the year of the great railway strikes, it was joined by the International

Firemen's Union, an organization without any fraternal or insurance features. In spite of this amalgamation, however, the growth of the Brotherhood was very slow. Indeed, so unsatisfactory was the condition of affairs that in 1879 the order took an unusual step. "So bitter was the continued opposition of railroad officials at this time," relates the chronicler of the Brotherhood (in some sections of the country it resulted in the disbandment of the lodges and the depletion of membership) "that it was decided, in order to remove the cause of such opposition, to eliminate the protective feature of the organization. With a view to this end a resolution was adopted ignoring strikes." This is one of the few recorded retreats of militant trade unionism. The treasury of the Brotherhood was so depleted that it was obliged to call upon local lodges for donations. By 1885, however, the order had sufficiently recovered to assume again the functions of a labor union in addition to its fraternal and beneficiary obligations. The days of its greatest hardships were over, although the historic strike on the Burlington lines that lasted virtually throughout the year 1888 and the Pullman strike in 1894 wrought a severe strain upon its staying powers. In 1906 the enginemen were incorporated into the order, and thenceforth the membership grew rapidly. In 1913 a joint agreement was effected with the Brotherhood of Locomotive Engineers whereby the two organizations could work together "on a labor union basis." Today men operating electric engines or motor or gas cars on lines using electricity are eligible for membership, if they are otherwise qualified. This arrangement does not interfere with unions already established on interurban lines.

The leadership of this order of firemen has been less continuous, though scarcely less conspicuous, than that of the other brotherhoods. Before 1886 the Grand Secretary and Treasurer was invested with greater authority than the grand master, and in this position Eugene V. Debs, who served from 1881 to 1892, and Frank W. Arnold, who served from 1893 to 1903, were potent in shaping the policies of the Union. There have been seven grand masters and one president (the name now used to designate the chief officer) since 1874. Of these leaders Frank P. Sargent served from 1886 until 1892, when he was appointed Commissioner General of Immigration by President Roosevelt. Since 1909, William S. Carter has been president of the Brotherhood. Born in Texas in 1859, he began railroading at nineteen years of age and served in turn as fireman, baggageman, and engineer. Before his election to the editorship of the *Firemen's Magazine*, he held various minor offices in local lodges. Since 1894 he has served the order successively as editor, grand secretary and treasurer, and president. To his position he has brought an intimate knowledge of the affairs of the Union as well as a varied experience in practical railroading. Upon the entrance of America into the Great War, President Wilson appointed him Director of the Division of Labor of the United States Railway Administration.

Of the government and policy of the firemen's union President Carter remarked:

This Brotherhood may be compared to a state in a republic of railway unions, maintaining almost complete autonomy in its own affairs yet uniting with other railway brotherhoods in matters of mutual concern and in common defense. It is true that these railway brotherhoods carry the principle of home rule to great lengths and have acknowledged no common head, and by this have invited the criticism from those who believe . . . that only in one "big" union can railway employees hope for improved working condition. . . . That in union there is strength, no one will deny, but in any confederation of forces there must be an exchange of individual rights for this collective power. There is a point in the combining of working people in labor unions where the loss of individual rights is not compensated by the increased power of the masses of workers.

In the cautious working out of this principle, the firemen have prospered after the manner of their colleagues in the other brotherhoods. Their membership embraces the large majority of their craft. From the date of the establishment of their beneficiary fund to 1918 a total of $21,860,103.00 has been paid in death and disability claims and in 1918 the amount so paid was $1,538,207.00. The *Firemen's Magazine*, established in 1876 and now published from headquarters in Cleveland, is indicative of the ambitions of the membership, for its avowed aim is to "make a specialty of educational matter for locomotive enginemen and other railroad employees." An attempt was even made in 1908 to conduct a correspondence school, under the supervision of the editor and manager of the magazine, but after three years this project was discontinued because it could not be made self-supporting.

The youngest of the railway labor organizations is the Brotherhood of Trainmen, organized in September, 1883, at Oneonta, New York. Its early years were lean and filled with bickerings and doubts, and it was not until S. E. Wilkinson was elected grand master in 1885 that it assumed an important rôle in labor organizations. Wilkinson was one of those big, rough and ready men, with a natural aptitude for leadership, who occasionally emerge from the mass. He preferred railroading to schooling and spent more time in the train sheds of his native town of Monroeville, Ohio, than he did at school. At twelve years of age he ran away to join the Union Army, in which he served as an orderly until the end of the war. He then followed his natural bent, became a switchman and later a brakeman, was a charter member of the Brotherhood, and, when its outlook was least encouraging, became its Grand Master. At once under his leadership the organization became aggressive.

The conditions under which trainmen worked were far from satisfactory. At that time, in the Eastern field, the pay of a brakeman was between $1.50 and $2 a day in the freight service, $45 a month in the passenger service, and $50 a month for yard service. In the Southern territory, the wages were very much lower and in the Western about $5 per month higher. The runs in the different sections of the country were not equalized; there was no limit to the number of hours called a day's work; overtime and preparatory time were not counted in; and there were many complaints of arbitrary treatment of trainmen by their superiors. Wilkinson set to work to remedy the wage situation first. Almost at once he brought about the adoption of the principle of collective bargaining for trainmen and yardmen. By 1895, when he relinquished his office, the majority of the railways in the United States and Canada had working agreements with their train and yard service men. Wages had been raised, twelve hours or less and one hundred miles or less became recognized as a daily measure of service, and overtime was paid extra.

The panic of 1893 hit the railway service very hard. There followed many strikes engineered by the American Railway Union, a radical organization which carried its ideas of violence so far that it wrecked not only itself but brought the newer and conservative Brotherhoods to the verge of ruin. It was during this period of strain that, in 1895, P. H. Morrissey was chosen Grand Master of the Trainmen. With a varied training in railroading, in insurance, and in labor organization work, Morrissey was in many ways the antithesis of his predecessors who had, in a powerful and brusque way, prepared the ground for his analytical and judicial leadership. He was unusually well informed on all matters pertaining to railroad operations, earnings, and conditions of employment, and on general economic conditions. This knowledge, together with his forcefulness, tact, parliamentary ability, and rare good judgment, soon made him the spokesman of all the railway Brotherhoods in their joint conferences and their leader before the public. He was not afraid to take the unpopular side of a cause, cared nothing for mere temporary advantages, and had the gift of inspiring confidence.

When Morrissey assumed the leadership of the Trainmen, their order had lost 10,000 members in two years and was about $200,000 in debt. The panic had produced unemployment and distrust, and the violent reprisals of the American Railway Union had reaped a harvest of bitterness and disloyalty. During his fifteen years of service until he retired in 1909, Morrissey saw his order rejuvenated and virtually reconstructed, the work of the men standardized in the greater part of the country, slight increases of pay given to the freight and passenger men, and very substantial increases granted to the yard men. But his greatest service to his order was in thoroughly establishing it in the public confidence.

He was succeeded by William G. Lee, who had served in many subordinate offices in local lodges before he had been chosen First Vice-Grand Master in 1895. For fifteen years he was a faithful understudy to Morrissey whose policy he has continued in a characteristically fearless and thoroughgoing manner. When he assumed the presidency of the order, he obtained a ten-hour day in the Eastern territory for all train and yard men, together with a slight increase in pay for all classes fixed on the ten-hour basis. The ten-hour day was now adopted in Western territory where it had not already been put into effect. The Southern territory, however, held out until 1912, when a general advance on all Southern railroads, with one exception, brought the freight and passenger men to a somewhat higher level of wages than existed in other parts of the country. In the following year the East and the West raised their wages so that finally a fairly level rate prevailed throughout the United States. In the movement for the eight-hour day which culminated in the passage of the Adamson Law by Congress, Lee and his order took a prominent part. In 1919 the Trainmen had

$253,000,000 insurance in force, and up to that year had paid out $42,500,000 in claims. Of this latter amount $3,604,000 was paid out in 1918, one-half of which was attributed to the influenza epidemic.

Much of the success and power of the railroad Brotherhoods is due to the character of their members as well as to able leadership. The editor of a leading newspaper has recently written: "The impelling power behind every one of these organizations is the membership. I say this without detracting from the executive or administrative abilities of the men who have been at the head of these organizations, for their influence has been most potent in carrying out the will of their several organizations. But whatever is done is first decided upon by the men and it is then put up to their chief executive officers for their direction."

With a membership of 375,000 uniformly clean and competent, so well captained and so well fortified financially by insurance, benefit, and other funds, it is little wonder that the Brotherhoods have reached a permanent place in the railroad industry. Their progressive power can be discerned in Federal legislation pertaining to arbitration and labor conditions in interstate carriers. In 1888 an act was passed providing that, in cases of railway labor disputes, the President might appoint two investigators who, with the United States Commission of Labor, should form a board to investigate the controversy and recommend "the best means for adjusting it." But as they were empowered to produce only findings and not to render decisions, the law remained a dead letter, without having a single case brought up under it. It was superseded in 1898 by the Erdman Act, which provided that certain Federal officials should act as mediators and that, in case they failed, a Board of Arbitrators was to be appointed whose word should be binding for a certain period of time and from whose decisions appeal could be taken to the Federal courts. Of the hundreds of disputes which occurred during the first eight years of the existence of this statute, only one was brought under the mechanism of the law. Federal arbitration was not popular. In 1905, however, a rather sudden change came over the situation. Over sixty cases were brought under the Erdman Act in about eight years. In 1913 the Newlands Law was passed providing for a permanent Board of Mediation and Conciliation, by which over sixty controversies have been adjusted.

The increase of brotherhood influence which

such legislation represents was accompanied by a consolidation in power. At first the Brotherhoods operated by railway systems or as individual orders. Later on they united into districts, all the Brotherhoods of a given district coöperating in their demands. Finally the coöperation of all the Brotherhoods in the United States on all the railway systems was effected. This larger organization came clearly to light in 1912, when the Brotherhoods submitted their disputes to the board of arbitration. This step was hailed by the public as going a long way towards the settlement of labor disputes by arbitral boards.

The latest victory of the Brotherhoods, however, has shaken public confidence and has ushered in a new era of brotherhood influence and Federal interference in railroad matters. In 1916, the four Brotherhoods threatened to strike. The mode of reckoning pay — whether upon an eight-hour or a longer day — was the subject of contention. The Department of Labor, through the Federal Conciliation Board, tried in vain to bring the opponents together. Even President Wilson's efforts to bring about an agreement proved futile. The roads agreed to arbitrate all the points, allowing the President to name the arbitrators; but the

Brotherhoods, probably realizing their temporary strategic advantage, refused point-blank to arbitrate. When the President tried to persuade the roads to yield the eight-hour day, they replied that it was a proper subject for arbitration.

Instead of standing firmly on the principle of arbitration, the President chose to go before Congress, on the afternoon of the 29th of August, and ask, first, for a reorganization of the Interstate Commerce Commission; second, for legal recognition of the eight-hour day for interstate carriers; third, for power to appoint a commission to observe the operation of the eight-hour day for a stated time; fourth, for reopening the question of an increase in freight rates to meet the enlarged cost of operation; fifth, for a law declaring railway strikes and lockouts unlawful until a public investigation could be made; sixth, for authorization to operate the roads in case of military necessity.

The strike was planned to fall on the expectant populace, scurrying home from their vacations, on the 4th of September. On the 1st of September an eight-hour bill, providing also for the appointment of a board of observation, was rushed through the House; on the following day it was hastened through the staid Senate; and on the third it received the President's signature.[1] The other recommendations of the President were made to await the pleasure of Congress and the unions. To the suggestion that railway strikes be made unlawful until their causes are disclosed the Brotherhoods were absolutely opposed.

Many readjustments were involved in launching the eight-hour law, and in March, 1917, the Brotherhoods again threatened to strike. The President sent a committee, including the Secretary of the Interior and the Secretary of Labor, to urge the parties to come to an agreement. On the 19th of March, the Supreme Court upheld the validity of the law, and the trouble subsided. But in the following November, after the declaration of war, clouds reappeared on the horizon, and again the unions refused the Government's suggestion of arbitration. Under war pressure, however, the Brotherhoods finally consented to hold their grievance in abeyance.

The haste with which the eight-hour law was enacted, and the omission of the vital balance suggested by the President appeared to many citizens

[1] This was on Sunday. In order to obviate any objection as to the legality of the signature the President signed the bill again on the following Tuesday, the intervening Monday being Labor Day.

to be a holdup of Congress, and the nearness of the presidential election suggested that a political motive was not absent. The fact that in the ensuing presidential election, Ohio, the home of the Brotherhoods, swung from the Republican to the Democratic column, did not dispel this suspicion from the public mind. Throughout this maneuver it was apparent that the unions were very confident, but whether because of a prearranged pact, or because of a full treasury, or because of a feeling that the public was with them, or because of the opposite belief that the public feared them, must be left to individual conjecture. None the less, the public realized that the principle of arbitration had given way to the principle of coercion.

Soon after the United States had entered the Great War, the Government, under authority of an act of Congress, took over the management of all the interstate railroads, and the nation was launched upon a vast experiment destined to test the capacities of all the parties concerned. The dispute over wages that had been temporarily quieted by the Adamson Law broke out afresh until settled by the famous *Order No. 27*, issued by William G. McAdoo, the Director General of Railroads, and providing a substantial readjustment of wages and hours. In the spring of 1919 another large wage increase was granted to the men by Director General Hines, who succeeded McAdoo. Meanwhile the Brotherhoods, through their counsel, laid before the congressional committee a plan for the government ownership and joint operation of the roads, known as the Plumb plan, and the American people are now face to face with an issue which will bring to a head the **paramount** question of the relation of employees on government works **to the** Government and to the general public.

CHAPTER VIII

ISSUES AND WARFARE

THERE has been an enormous expansion in the demands of the unions since the early days of the Philadelphia cordwainers; yet these demands involve the same fundamental issues regarding hours, wages, and the closed shop. Most unions, when all persiflage is set aside, are primarily organized for business — the business of looking after their own interests. Their treasury is a war chest rather than an insurance fund. As a benevolent organization, the American union is far behind the British union with its highly developed Friendly Societies.

The establishment of a standard rate of wages is perhaps, as the United States Industrial Commission reported in 1901, "the primary object of trade union policy." The most promising method of adjusting the wage contract is by the collective trade agreement. The mechanism of the union has made possible collective bargaining, and in numerous trades wages and other conditions are now adjusted by this method. One of the earliest of these agreements was effected by the Iron Molders' Union in 1891 and has been annually renewed. The coal operatives, too, for a number of years have signed a wage agreement with their miners, and the many local difficulties and differences have been ingeniously and successfully met. The great railroads have, likewise, for many years made periodical contracts with the railway Brotherhoods. The glove-makers, cigar-makers, and, in many localities, workers in the building trades and on street-railway systems have the advantage of similar collective agreements. In 1900 the American Newspaper Publishers Association and the International Typographical Union, after many years of stubborn fighting merged their numerous differences in a trade contract to be in effect for one year. This experiment proved so successful that the agreement has since then been renewed for five-year periods. In 1915 a bitter strike of the garment makers in New York City was ended by a "protocol." The principle of collective agreement has become so prevalent that the Massachusetts Bureau of Labor believes that it "is being accepted with increasing favor by both employers and employees," and John Mitchell, speaking from wide experience and an intimate knowledge of conditions, says that "the hope of future peace in the industrial world lies in the trade agreement." These agreements are growing in complexity, and today they embrace not only questions of wages and hours but also methods for adjusting all the differences which may arise between the parties to the bargain.

The very success of collective bargaining hinges upon the solidarity and integrity of the union which makes the bargain. A union capable of enforcing an agreement is a necessary antecedent condition to such a contract. With this fact in mind, one can believe that John Mitchell was not unduly sanguine in stating that "the tendency is toward the growth of compulsory membership . . . and the time will doubtless come when this compulsion will be as general and will be considered as little of a grievance as the compulsory attendance of children at school." There are certain industries so well centralized, however, that their coercive power is greater than that of the labor union, and these have maintained a consistent hostility to the closed shop. The question of the closed shop is, indeed, the most stubborn issue confronting the union.

The principle involves the employment of only union men in a shop; it means a monopoly of jobs by members of the union. The issue is as old as the unions themselves and as perplexing as human nature. As early as 1806 it was contended for by the Philadelphia cordwainers and by 1850 it had become an established union policy. While wages and hours are now, in the greater industrial fields, the subject of a collective contract, this question of union monopoly is still open, though there has been some progress towards an adjustment. Wherever the trade agreement provides for a closed shop, the union, through its proper committees and officers, assumes at least part of the responsibility of the discipline. The agreement also includes methods for arbitrating differences. The acid test of the union is its capacity to live up to this trade agreement.

For the purpose of forcing its policies upon its employers and society the unions have resorted to the strike and picketing, the boycott, and the union label. When violence occurs, it usually is the concomitant of a strike; but violence unaccompanied by a strike is sometimes used as a union weapon.

The strike is the oldest and most spectacular weapon in the hands of labor. For many years it was thought a necessary concomitant of machine industry. The strike, however, antedates machinery and was a practical method of protest long before there were unions. Men in a shop simply agreed not to work further and walked out. The earliest strike in the United States, as disclosed by the United States Department of Labor occurred in 1741 among the journeymen bakers in New York City. In 1792 the cordwainers of Philadelphia struck. By 1834 strikes were so prevalent that the New York *Daily Advertiser* declared them to be "all the fashion." These demonstrations were all small affairs compared with the strikes that disorganized industry after the Civil War or those that swept the country in successive waves in the late seventies, the eighties, and the nineties. The United States Bureau of Labor has tabulated the strike statistics for the twenty-five year period from 1881 to 1905. This list discloses the fact that 38,303 strikes and lockouts occurred, involving 199,954 establishments and 7,444,279 employees. About 2,000,000 other employees were thrown out of work as an indirect result. In 1894, the year of the great Pullman strike, 610,425 men were out of work at one time; and 659,792 in 1902. How much time and money these ten million wage-earners lost, and their employers lost, and society lost, can never be computed, nor how much nervous energy was wasted, good will thrown to the winds, and mutual suspicion created.

The increase of union influence is apparent, for recognition of the union has become more frequently a cause for strikes.[1] Moreover, while the unions were responsible for about 47 per cent of the strikes in 1881, they had originated, directly or indirectly, 75 per cent in 1905. More significant, indeed, is the fact that striking is a growing habit. In 1903, for instance, there were 3494 strikes, an average of about ten a day.

Preparedness is the watchword of the Unions in this warfare. They have generals and captains, a war chest and relief committees, as well as publicity agents and sympathy scouts whose duty it is to enlist the interest of the public. Usually the leaders of the unions are conservative and deprecate

---

[1] The cause of the strikes tabulated by the Bureau of Labor is shown in the following table of percentages:

	1881	1891	1901	1905
For increase of wages:	61	27	29	32
Against reduction of wages:	10	11	4	5
For reduction in hours:	3	5	7	5
Recognition of Union:	6	14	28	31

violence. But a strike by its very nature offers
an opportunity to the lawless.   The destruction of
property and the coercion of workmen have been
so prevalent in the past that, in the public mind,
violence has become universally associated with
strikes. Judge Jenkins, of the United States Circuit
Court, declared, in a leading case, that "a strike
without violence would equal the representation of
Hamlet with the part of Hamlet omitted." Justice
Brewer of the United States Supreme Court said
that "the common rule as to strikes" is not only
for the workers to quit but to "forcibly prevent
others from taking their place." Historic examples
involving violence of this sort are the great railway
strikes of 1877, when Pittsburgh, Reading, Cincinnati, Chicago, and Buffalo were mob-ridden; the
strike of the steel-workers at Homestead, Pennsylvania, in 1892; the Pullman strike of 1894, when
President Cleveland sent Federal troops to Chicago;
the great anthracite strike of 1902, which the Federal Commission characterized as "stained with
a record of riot and bloodshed"; the civil war in the
Colorado and Idaho mining regions, where the Western Federation of Miners battled with the militia
and Federal troops; the dynamite outrages, per-
petrated by the structural iron workers, stretching

across the entire country, and reaching a dastardly climax in the dynamiting of the Los Angeles *Times* building on October 1, 1910, in which some twenty men were killed. The recoil from this outrage was the severest blow which organized labor has received in America. John J. McNamara, Secretary of the Structural Iron Workers' Association, and his brother James were indicted for murder. After the trial was staged and the eyes of the nation were upon it, the public was shocked and the hopes of labor unionists were shattered by the confessions of the principals. In March, 1912, a Federal Grand Jury at Indianapolis returned fifty-four indictments against officers and members of the same union for participation in dynamite outrages that had occurred during the six years in many parts of the country, with a toll of over one hundred lives and the destruction of property valued at many millions of dollars. Among those indicted was the president of the International Association of Bridge and Structural Iron Workers. Most of the defendants were sentenced to various terms in the penitentiary.

The records of this industrial warfare are replete with lesser battles where thuggery joined hands with desperation in the struggle for wages.

Evidence is not wanting that local leaders have frequently incited their men to commit acts of violence in order to impress the public with their earnestness. It is not an inviting picture, this matching of the sullen violence of the mob against the sullen vigilance of the corporation. Yet such methods have not always been used, for the union has done much to systematize this guerrilla warfare. It has matched the ingenuity and the resolution of the employer, backed by his detectives and professional strike-breakers; it has perfected its organization so that the blow of a whistle or the mere uplifting of a hand can silence a great mill. Some of the notable strikes have been managed with rare skill and diplomacy. Some careful observers, indeed, are inclined to the opinion that the amount of violence that takes place in the average strike has been grossly exaggerated. They maintain that, considering the great number of strikes, the earnestness with which they are fought, the opportunity they offer to the lawless, and the vast range of territory they cover, the amount of damage to property and person is unusually small and that the public, through sensational newspaper reports of one or two acts of violence, is led to an exaggerated opinion of its prevalence.

It must be admitted, however, that the wisdom and conservatism of the national labor leaders is neutralized by their lack of authority in their particular organization. A large price is paid for the autonomy that permits the local unions to declare strikes without the sanction of the general officers. There are only a few unions, perhaps half a dozen, in which a local can be expelled for striking contrary to the wish of the national officers. In the United Mine Workers' Union, for example, the local must secure the consent of the district officers and national president, or, if these disagree, of the executive board, before it can declare a strike. The tendency to strike on the spur of the moment is much more marked among the newer unions than among the older ones, which have perfected their strike machinery through much experience and have learned the cost of hasty and unjustified action.

A less conspicuous but none the less effective weapon in the hands of labor is the boycott,[1] which is carried by some of the unions to a terrible

[1] In 1880, Lord Erne, an absentee Irish landlord, sent Captain Boycott to Connemara to subdue his irate tenants. The people of the region refused to have any intercourse whatever with the agent or his family. And social and business ostracism has since been known as the boycott.

12

perfection. It reached its greatest power in the decade between 1881 and 1891. Though it was aimed at a great variety of industries, it seemed to be peculiarly effective in the theater, hotel, restaurant, and publishing business, and in the clothing and cigar trades. For sheer arbitrary coerciveness, nothing in the armory of the union is so effective as the boycott. A flourishing business finds its trade gone overnight. Leading customers withdraw their patronage at the union's threat. The alert picket is the harbinger of ruin, and the union black list is as fraught with threat as the black hand.

The New York Bureau of Statistics of Labor has shown that during the period of eight years between 1885 and 1892 there were 1352 boycotts in New York State alone. A sort of terrorism spread among the tradespeople of the cities. But the unions went too far. Instances of gross unfairness aroused public sympathy against the boycotters. In New York City, for instance, a Mrs. Grey operated a small bakery with nonunion help. Upon her refusal to unionize her shop at the command of the walking delegate, her customers were sent the usual boycott notice, and pickets were posted. Her delivery wagons were followed, and her customers were threatened. Grocers selling her bread were systematically boycotted. All this persecution merely aroused public sympathy for Mrs. Grey, and she found her bread becoming immensely popular. The boycotters then demanded $2500 for paying their boycott expenses. When news of this attempt at extortion was made public, it heightened the tide of sympathy, the courts took up the matter, and the boycott failed. The *New York Boycotter*, a journal devoted to this form of coercion, declared: "In boycotting we believe it to be legitimate to strike a man financially, socially, or politically. We believe in hitting him where it will hurt the most; we believe in remorselessly crowding him to the wall; but when he is down, instead of striking him, we would lift him up and stand him once more on his feet." When the boycott thus enlisted the aid of blackmail, it was doomed in the public esteem. Boycott indictments multiplied, and in one year in New York City alone, over one hundred leaders of such attempts at coercion were sentenced to imprisonment.

The boycott, however, was not laid aside as a necessary weapon of organized labor because it had been abused by corrupt or overzealous unionists, nor because it had been declared illegal by the courts. All the resources of the more conservative

unions and of the American Federation of Labor
have been enlisted to make it effective in extreme
instances where the strike has failed. This application of the method can best be illustrated by the
two most important cases of boycott in our history,
the Buck's Stove and Range case and the Danbury
Hatters' case. Both were fought through the Federal courts, with the defendants backed by the American Federation and opposed by the Anti-Boycott
Association, a federation of employers.

The Buck's Stove and Range Company of St.
Louis incurred the displeasure of the Metal Polishers' Union by insisting upon a ten-hour day. On
August 27, 1906, at five o'clock in the afternoon, on
a prearranged signal, the employees walked out.
They returned to work the next morning and all
were permitted to take their accustomed places
except those who had given the signal. They were
discharged. At five o'clock that afternoon the
men put aside their work, and the following morning reappeared. Again the men who had given the
signal were discharged, and the rest went to work.
The union then sent notice to the foreman that the
discharged men must be reinstated or that all would
quit. A strike ensued which soon led to a boycott
of national proportions. It spread from the local

to the St. Louis Central Trades and Labor Union and to the Metal Polishers' Union. In 1907 the executive council of the American Federation of Labor officially placed the Buck's Stove and Range Company on the unfair list and gave this action wide and conspicuous circulation in *The Federationist*. This boycott received further impetus from the action of the Mine Workers, who in their Annual Convention resolved that the Buck's Stove and Range Company be put on the unfair list and that "any member of the United Mine Workers of America purchasing a stove of above make be fined $5.00 and failing to pay the same be expelled from the organization."

Espionage became so efficient and letters from old customers withdrawing patronage became so numerous and came from so wide a range of territory that the company found itself rapidly nearing ruin. An injunction was secured, enjoining the American Federation from blacklisting the company. The labor journals circumvented this mandate by publishing in display type the statement that "It is unlawful for the American Federation of Labor to boycott Buck's Stoves and Ranges," and then in small type adroitly recited the news of the court's decision in such a way that the reader would see at a glance that the company was under union ban. These evasions of the court's order were interpreted as contempt, and in punishment the officers of the Federation were sentenced to imprisonment — Frank Morrison for six months, John Mitchell for nine months, Samuel Gompers for twelve months. But a technicality intervened between the leaders and the cells awaiting them. The public throughout the country had followed the course of this case with mingled feelings of sympathy and disfavor, and though the boycott had never met with popular approval, on the whole the public was relieved to learn that the jail-sentences were not to be served.

The Danbury Hatters' boycott was brought on in 1903 by the attempt of the Hatters' Union to make a closed shop of a manufacturing concern in Danbury, Connecticut. The unions moved upon Danbury, flushed with two recent victories — one in Philadelphia, where an important hat factory had agreed to the closed shop after spending some $40,000 in fighting, and another at Orange, New Jersey, where a manufacturer had spent $25,000. But as the Danbury concern was determined to fight the union, in 1902 a nation-wide boycott was declared. The company then brought suit against members of the union in the United States District Court. Injunction proceedings reached the Supreme Court of the United States on a demurrer, and in February, 1908, the court declared that the Sherman Anti-Trust Law forbade interstate boycotts. The case then returned to the original court for trial. Testimony was taken in many States, and after a trial lasting twelve weeks the jury assessed the damages to the plaintiff at $74,000. On account of error, the case was remanded for re-trial in 1911. At the second trial the jury gave the plaintiff a verdict for $80,000, the full amount asked. According to the law, this amount was trebled, leaving the judgment, with costs added, at $252,000. The Supreme Court having sustained the verdict, the puzzling question of how to collect it arose. As such funds as the union had were invulnerable to process, the savings bank accounts of the individual defendants were attached. The union insisted that the defendants were not taxable for accrued interest, and the United States Supreme Court, now appealed to for a third time, sustained the plaintiff's contention. In this manner $60,000 were obtained. Foreclosure proceedings were then begun against one hundred and forty homes belonging to union men in the towns of Danbury, Norwalk, and Bethel. The union boasted that this sale would prove only an incubus to the purchasers, for no one would dare occupy the houses sold under such circumstances. In the meantime the American Federation, which had financed the litigation, undertook to raise the needed sum by voluntary collection and made Gompers's birthday the occasion for a gift to the Danbury local. The Federation insisted that the houses be sold on foreclosure and that the collected money be used not as a prior settlement but as an indemnity to the individuals thus deprived of their homes. Rancor gave way to reason, however, and just before the day fixed for the foreclosure sale the matter was settled. In all, $235,000 was paid in damages by the union to the company. In the fourteen years during which this contest was waged, about forty defendants, one of the plaintiffs, and eight judges who had passed on the controversy, died. The outcome served as a spur to the Federation in hastening through Congress the Clayton bill of 1914, designed to place labor unions beyond the reach of the anti-trust laws.

The union label has in more recent years achieved importance as a weapon in union warfare. This is a mark or device denoting a union-made article.

It might be termed a sort of labor union trade-mark. Union men are admonished to favor the goods so marked, but it was not until national organizations were highly perfected that the label could become of much practical value. It is a device of American invention and was first used by the cigar makers in 1874. In 1880 their national body adopted the now familiar blue label and, with great skill and perseverance and at a considerable outlay of money, has pushed its union-made ware, in the face of sweat-shop competition, of the introduction of cigar making machinery, and of fraudulent imitation. Gradually other unions making products of common consumption adopted labels. Conspicuous among these were the garment makers, the hat makers, the shoe makers, and the brewery workers. As the value of the label manifestly depends upon the trade it entices, the unions are careful to emphasize the sanitary conditions and good workmanship which a label represents.

The application of the label is being rapidly extended. Building materials are now in many large cities under label domination. In Chicago the bricklayers have for over fifteen years been able to force the builders to use only union-label brick, and the carpenters have forced the contractors to use only material from union mills. There is practically no limit to this form of mandatory boycott. The barbers, retail clerks, hotel employees, and butcher workmen hang union cards in their places of employment or wear badges as insignia of union loyalty. As these labels do not come under the protection of the United States trade-mark laws, the unions have not infrequently been forced to bring suits against counterfeiters.

Finally, in their efforts to fortify themselves against undue increase in the rate of production or "speeding up," against the inrush of new machinery, and against the debilitating alternation of rush work and no work, the unions have attempted to restrict the output. The United States Industrial Commission reported in 1901 that "there has always been a strong tendency among labor organizations to discourage exertion beyond a certain limit. The tendency does not express itself in formal rules. On the contrary, it appears chiefly in the silent, or at least informal pressure of working class opinion." Some unions have rules, others a distinct understanding, on the subject of a normal day's work, and some discourage piecework. But it is difficult to determine how far this policy has been carried in application. Carroll D. Wright, in a special report as United States Commissioner of Labor in 1904, said that "unions in some cases fix a limit to the amount of work a workman may perform a day. Usually it is a secret understanding, but sometimes, when the union is strong, no concealment is made." His report mentioned several trades, including the building trades, in which this curtailment is prevalent.

The course of this industrial warfare between the unions and the employers has been replete with sordid details of selfishness, corruption, hatred, suspicion, and malice. In every community the strike or the boycott has been an ominous visitant, leaving in its trail a social bitterness which even time finds it difficult to efface. In the great cities and the factory towns, the constant repetition of labor struggles has created centers of perennial discontent which are sources of never-ending reprisals. In spite of individual injustice, however, one can discern in the larger movements a current setting towards a collective justice and a communal ideal which society in self-defense is imposing upon the combatants.

CHAPTER IX

IT was not to be expected that the field of organized labor would be left undisputed to the moderation of the trade union after its triumph over the extreme methods of the Knights of Labor. The public, however, did not anticipate the revolutionary ideal which again sought to inflame industrial unionism. After the decadence of the older type of the industrial union several conditions manifested themselves which now, in retrospect, appear to have encouraged the violent militants who call themselves the Industrial Workers of the World.

First of all, there took place in Europe the rise of syndicalism with its adoption of sympathetic strikes as one of its methods. Syndicalism flourished especially in France, where from its inception the alert French mind had shaped for it a philosophy of violence, whose subtlest exponent was Georges Sorel. *The Socialist Future of Trade*

188

Unions, which he published in 1897, was an early exposition of his views, but his *Reflections upon Violence* in 1908 is the best known of his contributions to this newer doctrine. With true Gallic fervor, the French workingman had sought to translate his philosophy into action, and in 1906 undertook, with the aid of a revolutionary organization known as the *Confédération Général du Travail*, a series of strikes which culminated in the railroad and post office strike of 1909. All these uprisings — for they were in reality more than strikes — were characterized by extreme language, by violent action, and by impressive public demonstrations. In Italy, Spain, Norway, and Belgium, the syndicalists were also active. Their partiality to violent methods attracted general attention in Europe and appealed to that small group of American labor leaders whose experience in the Western Federation of Miners had taught them the value of dynamite as a press agent.

In the meantime material was being gathered for a new outbreak in the United States. The casual laborers had greatly increased in numbers, especially in the West. These migratory workingmen — the "hobo miners," the "hobo lumberjacks," the "blanket stiffs," of colloquial speech —

wander about the country in search of work. They rarely have ties of family and seldom ties of locality. About one-half of these wanderers are American born. They are to be described with precision as "floaters." Their range of operations includes the wheat regions west of the Mississippi, the iron mines of Michigan and Minnesota, the mines and forests of Idaho, Montana, Colorado, Washington, and Oregon, and the fields of California and Arizona. They prefer to winter in the cities, but, as their only refuge is the bunk lodging house, they increase the social problem in New York, Chicago, San Francisco, and other centers of the unemployed. Many of these migrants never were skilled workers; but a considerable portion of them have been forced down into the ranks of the unskilled by the inevitable tragedies of prolonged unemployment. Such men lend a willing ear to the labor agitator. The exact number in this wandering class is not known. The railroad companies have estimated that at a given time there have been 500,000 hobos trying to beat their way from place to place. Unquestionably a large percentage of the 23,964 trespassers killed and of the 25,236 injured on railway rights of way from 1901 to 1904 belonged to this class.

It is not alone these drifters, however, who because of their irresponsibility and their hostility toward society became easy victims to the industrial organizer. The great mass of unskilled workers in the factory towns proved quite as tempting to the propagandist. Among laborers of this class, wages are the lowest and living conditions the most uninviting. Moreover, this group forms the industrial reservoir which receives the settlings of the most recent European and Asiatic immigration. These people have a standard of living and conceptions of political and individual freedom which are at variance with American traditions. Though their employment is steadier than that of the migratory laborer, and though they often have ties of family and other stabilizing responsibilities, their lives are subject to periods of unemployment, and these fluctuations serve to feed their innate restlessness. They are, in quite the literal sense of the word, American proletarians. They are more volatile than any European proletarian, for they have learned the lesson of migration, and they retain the socialistic and anarchistic philosophy of their European fellow-workers.

There were several attempts to organize casual labor after the decline of the Knights of Labor.

But it is difficult to arouse any sustained interest in industrial organizations among workingmen of this class. They lack the motive of members of a trade union, and the migratory character of such workers deprives their organization of stability. One industrial organization, however, has been of the greatest encouragement to the I. W. W. The Western Federation of Miners, which was organized at Butte, Montana, on May 15, 1893, has enjoyed a more turbulent history than any other American labor union. It was conceived in that spirit of rough resistance which local unions of miners, for some years before the amalgamation of the unions, had opposed to the ruthless and firm determination of the mine owners. In 1897, the president of the miners, after quoting the words of the Constitution of the United States giving citizens the right to bear arms, said: "This you should comply with immediately. Every union should have a rifle club. I strongly advise you to provide every member with the latest improved rifle which can be obtained from the factory at a nominal price. I entreat you to take action on this important question, so that in two years we can hear the inspiring music of the martial tread of 25,000 armed men in the ranks of labor."

This militant vision was fortunately never quite fulfilled. But armed strikers there were, by the thousands, and the gruesome details of their fight with mine owners in Colorado are set forth in a special report of the United States Commissioner of Labor in 1905. The use of dynamite became early associated with this warfare in Colorado. In 1903 a fatal explosion occurred in the Vindicator mine in Teller County, and serious disorders broke out in Telluride, the county seat of San Miguel County. In 1904 a cage lifting miners from the shaft in the Independence mine at Victor was dropped and fifteen men were killed. There were many minor outrages, isolated murders, "white cap" raids, infernal machines, deportations, black lists, and so on. In Montana and Idaho similar scenes were enacted and reached a climax in the murder of Governor Steunenberg of Idaho. Yet the union officers indicted for this murder were released by the trial jury.

Such was the preparatory school of the new unionism, which had its inception in several informal conferences held in Chicago. The first, attended by only six radical leaders, met in the autumn of 1904. The second, held in January, 1905, issued a manifesto attacking the trade unions, calling for a "new departure" in the labor movement, and inviting those who desired to join in organizing such a movement to "meet in convention in Chicago the 27th day of June, 1905." About two hundred persons responded to this appeal and organized the Industrial Workers of the World, almost unnoticed by the press of the day and scorned by the American Federation of Labor, whose official organ had called those in attendance at the second conference "engaged in the delectable work of trying to divert, pervert, and disrupt the labor movement of the country."

An overwhelming influence in this convention was wielded by the Western Federation of Miners and the Socialistic American Labor Union, two radical labor bodies which looked upon the trade unions as "union snobbery" and the "aristocracy of labor," and upon the American Federation as "the consummate flower of craft unionism" and "a combination of job trusts." They believed trade unionism wrong in principle. They discarded the principle of trade autonomy for the principle of laboring class solidarity, for, as one of their spokesmen said, "The industrial union, in contradistinction to the craft union, is that organization through which all its members in one industry, or in all industries if necessary, can act as a unit."

While this convention was united in denouncing the trade unions, it was not so unanimous in other matters, for the leaders were all veterans in those factional quarrels which characterize Socialists the world over. Eugene V. Debs, for example, was the hero of the Knights of Labor and had achieved wide notoriety during the Pullman strike by being imprisoned for contempt of court. William D. Haywood, popularly known as "Big Bill," received a rigorous training in the Western Federation of Miners. Daniel DeLeon, whose right name, the *American Federationist* alleged, was Daniel Loeb, was a university graduate and a vehement revolutionary, the leader of the Socialistic Labor party, and the editor of the *Daily People*. A. M. Simons, the leader of the Socialist party and the editor of the *Coming Nation*, was at swords' points with DeLeon. William E. Trautmann was the fluent spokesman of the anti-political faction. These men dominated the convention.

After some twelve days of discussion, they agreed upon a constitution which established six departments,[1] provided for a general executive

[1] 1. Agriculture, Land, Fisheries, and Water Products. 2. Mining. 3. Transportation and Communication. 4. Manufacturing and General Production. 5. Construction. 6. Public Service.

board with centralized powers, and at the same time left to the local and department organizations complete industrial autonomy. The I. W. W. in "the first constitution, crude and provisional as it was, made room for all the world's workers."[1] This was, indeed, the great object of the organization.

Whatever visions of world conquest the militants may at first have fostered were soon shattered by internal strife. There were unreconcilable elements in the body: those who regarded the political aspect as paramount and industrial unions as allies of socialism; those who regarded the forming of unions as paramount and politics as secondary; and those who regarded all forms of political activity as mere waste of energy. The first two groups were tucked under the wings of the Socialist party and the Socialist Labor party. The third group was frankly anarchistic and revolutionary. In the fourth annual convention the Socialist factions withdrew, established headquarters at Detroit, organized what is called the Detroit branch, and left the Chicago field to the revolutionists. So socialism "pure and simple," and what amounts to

[1] J. G. Brissenden, *The Launching of the Industrial Workers of the World*, page 41.

anarchism "pure and simple," fell out, after they had both agreed to disdain trade unionism "pure and simple."

This shift proved the great opportunity for Haywood and his disciples. Feeling himself now free of all political encumbrances, he gathered around him a small group of enthusiastic leaders, some of whom had a gift of diabolical intrigue, and with indomitable perseverance and zeal he set himself to seeking out the neglected, unskilled, and casual laborer. Within a few years he so dominated the movement that, in the public mind, the I. W. W. is associated with the Chicago branch and the Detroit faction is well-nigh forgotten.

As a preliminary to a survey of some of the battles that made the I. W. W. a symbol of terror in many communities it will be well to glance for a moment at the underlying doctrines of the organization. In a preamble now notorious it declared that "the working class and the employing class have nothing in common. There can be no peace so long as hunger and want are found among millions of working people, and the few who make up the employing class have all the good things of life. Between these two classes a struggle must go on until the workers of the world as a class take possession of the earth and the machinery of production and abolish the wage system."

This thesis is a declaration of war as well as a declaration of principles. The I. W. W. aims at nothing less than the complete overthrow of modern capitalism and the political structure which accompanies it. Emma Goldman, who prides herself on having received her knowledge of syndicalism "from actual contact" and not from books, says that "syndicalism repudiates and condemns the present industrial arrangement as unjust and criminal." Edward Hamond calls the labor contract "the sacred cow" of industrial idolatry and says that the aim of the I. W. W. is "the abolition of the wage system." And W. E. Trautmann affirms that "the industrial unionist holds that there can be no agreement with the employers of labor which the workers have to consider sacred and inviolable." In place of what they consider an unjust and universal capitalistic order they would establish a new society in which "the unions of the workers will own and manage all industries, regulate consumption, and administer the general social interests."

How is this contemplated revolution to be achieved? By the working classes themselves and not through political activity, for "one of the first principles of the I. W. W. is that political power rests on economic power. . . . It must gain control of the shops, ships, railways, mines, mills." And how is it to gain this all-embracing control? By persuading every worker to join the union, the "one great organization" which, according to Haywood, is to be "big enough to take in the black man, the white man; big enough to take in all nationalities — an organization that will be strong enough to obliterate state boundaries, to obliterate national boundaries. . . . We, the I. W. W., stand on our two feet, the class struggle and industrial unionism, and coolly say we want the whole earth." When the great union has become universal, it will simply take possession of its own, will "lock the employers out for good as owners and parasites, and give them a chance to become useful toilers." The resistance that will assuredly be made to this process of absorption is to be met by direct action, the general strike, and sabotage — a trinity of phrases imported from Europe, each one of special significance.

"The general strike means a stoppage of work," says Emma Goldman with naïve brevity. It was thought of long before the I. W. W. existed, but it has become the most valuable weapon in their arsenal. Their pamphlets contain many allusions to the great strikes in Belgium, Russia, Italy, France, Scandinavia, and other European countries, that were so widespread as to merit being called general. If all the workers can be induced to stop work, even for a very brief interval, such action would be regarded as the greatest possible manifestation of the "collective power of the producers."

Direct action, a term translated directly from the French, is more difficult to define. This method sets itself in opposition to the methods of the capitalist in retaining control of industry, which is spoken of as indirect action. Laws, machinery, credits, courts, and constabulary are indirect methods whereby the capitalist keeps possession of his property. The industrialist matches this with a direct method. For example, he engages in a passive strike, obeying rules so literally as to destroy both their utility and his work; or in an opportune strike, ceasing work suddenly when he knows his employer has orders that must be immediately filled; or in a temporary strike, quitting work one day and coming back the next. His weapon is organized opportunism, wielding an unexpected blow, and keeping the employer in a frenzy of fearful anticipation.

Finally, sabotage is a word that expresses the whole philosophy and practice of revolutionary labor. John Spargo, in his *Syndicalism, Industrial Unionism and Socialism*, traces the origin of the word to the dockers' union in London. Attempt after attempt had proved futile to win by strikes the demands of these unskilled workers. The men were quite at the end of their resources, when finally they hit upon the plan of "lying down on the job" or "soldiering." As a catchword they adopted the Scotch phrase *ca'canny*, to go slow or be careful not to do too much. As an example they pointed to the Chinese coolies who met a refusal of increased wages by cutting off a few inches from their shovels on the principle of "small pay, small work." He then goes on to say that "the idea was very easily extended. From the slowing up of the human worker to the slowing up of the iron worker, the machine, was an easy transition. Judiciously planned 'accidents' might easily create confusion for which no one could be blamed. A few 'mistakes' in handling cargoes might easily cost the employers far more than a small increase in wages would."

Some French syndicalists, visiting London, were greatly impressed with this new cunning. But as they had no ready translation for the Scottish *ca'- canny*, they ingeniously abstracted the same idea from the old French saying *Travailler à coups de sabots* — to work as if one had on wooden shoes — and sabotage thus became a new and expressive phrase in the labor war.

Armed with these weapons, Haywood and his henchmen moved forward. Not long after the first convention in 1905, they made their presence known at Goldfield, Nevada. Then they struck simultaneously at Youngstown, Ohio, and Portland, Oregon. The first battle, however, to attract general notice was at McKees Rocks, Pennsylvania, in 1909. In this warfare between the recently organized unskilled workers and the efficient state constabulary, the I. W. W. sent notice "that for every striker killed or injured by the cossacks, the life of a cossack will be exacted in return." And they collected their gruesome toll.

In 1912 occurred the historic strike in the mill town of Lawrence, Massachusetts. This affair was so adroitly managed by the organizers of the Workers that within a few weeks every newspaper of importance in America was publishing long descriptions of the new anarchism. Magazine writers, self-appointed reformers, delegations representing various organizations, three committees of the state legislature, the Governor's personal emissary, the United States Attorney, the United States Commissioner of Labor, and a congressional committee devoted their time to numerous investigations, thereby giving immense satisfaction to those obscure agitators who were lifted suddenly into the glare of universal notoriety, to the disgust of the town thus dragged into unenviable publicity, and to the discomfiture of the employers.

The legislature of Massachusetts had reduced the hours of work of women and children from fifty-six to fifty-four hours a week. Without making adequate announcement, the employers withheld two hours' pay from the weekly stipend. A large portion of the workers were foreigners, representing eighteen different nationalities, most of them with a wholly inadequate knowledge of English, and all of an inflammable temperament. When they found their pay short, a group marched through the mills, inciting others to join them, and the strike was on. The American Federation of Labor had paid little attention to these workers. There were some trade unions in the mills, but most of the workers were unorganized except for the fact that the I. W. W. had, about eight months before, gathered several hundred into an industrial union. Yet it does not appear that this union started the strike. It was a case of spontaneous combustion. No sooner had it begun, however, than Joseph J. Ettor, an I. W. W. organizer, hastened to take charge, and succeeded so well that within a few weeks he claimed 7000 members in his union. Ettor proved a crafty, resourceful general, quick in action, magnetic in personality, a linguist who could command his polyglot mob. He was also a successful press agent who exploited fully the unpalatable drinking water provided by the companies, the inadequate sewerage, the unpaved streets, and the practical destitution of many of the workers. The strikers made an attempt to send children to other towns so that they might be better cared for. After several groups had thus been taken away, the city of Lawrence interfered, claiming that many children had been sent without their parents' consent. On the 24th of February, when a group of forty children and their mothers gathered at the railway station to take a train for Philadelphia, the police after due warning refused to let them depart. It was then that the Federal

Government was called upon to take action. The strike committee telegraphed Congress: "Twenty-five thousand striking textile workers and citizens cf Lawrence protest against the hideous brutality with which the police handled the women and children of Lawrence this morning. Carrying out the illegal and original orders of the city marshal to prevent free citizens from sending their children out of the city, striking men were knocked down, women and mothers who were trying to protect their children from the onslaught of the police were attacked and clubbed." So widespread was the opinion that unnecessary brutality had taken place that petitions for an investigation poured in upon Congress from many States and numerous organizations.

The whole country was watching the situation. The hearings held by a congressional committee emphasized the stupidity of the employers in arbitrarily curtailing the wage, the inadequacy of the town government in handling the situation, and the cupidity of the I. W. W. leaders in taking advantage of the fears, the ignorance, the inflammability of the workers, and in creating a "terrorism which impregnated the whole city for days." Lawrence became a symbol. It stood for the American factory town; for municipal indifference and social neglect, for heterogeneity in population, for the tinder pile awaiting the incendiary match.

At Little Falls, New York, a strike occurred in the textile mills in October, 1912, as a result of a reduction of wages due to a fifty-four hour law. No organization was responsible for the strike, but no sooner had the operatives walked out than here also the I. W. W. appeared. The leaders ordered every striker to do something which would involve arrest in order to choke the local jail and the courts. The state authorities investigating the situation reported that "all of those on strike were foreigners and few, if any, could speak or understand the English language, complete control of the strike being in the hands of the I. W. W."

In February, 1913, about 15,000 employees in the rubber works at Akron, Ohio, struck. The introduction of machinery into the manufacture of automobile tires caused a reduction in the piece-work rate in certain shops. One of the companies posted a notice on the 10th of February that this reduction would take effect immediately. No time was given for conference, and it was this sudden arbitrary act which precipitated all the discontent lurking for a long time in the background; and the employees walked out. The legislative investigating committee reported "there was practically no organization existing among the rubber employees when the strike began. A small local of the Industrial Workers of the World comprised of between fifteen and fifty members had been formed. . . . Simultaneously with the beginning of the strike, organizers of the I. W. W. appeared on the ground inviting and urging the striking employees to unite with their organization." Many of these testified before the public authorities that they had not joined because they believed in the preachings of the organization but because "they hoped through collective action to increase their wages and improve their conditions of employment." The tactics of the strike leaders soon alienated the public, which had at first been inclined towards the strikers, and acts of violence led to the organization of a vigilance committee of one thousand citizens which warned the leaders to leave town.

In February, 1913, some 25,000 workers in the silk mills of Paterson, New Jersey, struck, and here again the I. W. W. repeated its maneuvers. Sympathetic meetings took place in New York and other cities. Daily "experience meetings" were held in Paterson and all sorts of devices were invented to maintain the fervor of the strikers. The leaders threatened to make Paterson a "howling wilderness," an "industrial graveyard," and "to wipe it off the map." This threat naturally arrayed the citizens against the strikers, over one thousand of whom were lodged in jail before the outbreak was over. Among the five ringleaders arrested and held for the grand jury were Elizabeth Gurley Flynn and Patrick Quinlan, whose trials attracted wide attention. Elizabeth Flynn, an appealing young widow scarcely over twenty-one, testified that she had begun her work as an organizer at the age of sixteen, that she had not incited strikers to violence but had only advised them to picket and to keep their hands in their pockets, "so that detectives could not put stones in them as they had done in other strikes." The jury disagreed and she was discharged. Quinlan, an unusually attractive young man, also a professional I. W. W. agitator, was found guilty of inciting to violence and was sentenced to a long term of imprisonment. After serving nine months he was freed because of a monster petition signed by some 20,000 sympathetic persons all over the United States. Clergymen, philanthropists, and prominent public men, were among the signers, as well as the jurors who convicted and the sheriff who locked up the defendant.

These cases served to fix further public attention upon the nature of the new movement and the sort of revivalists its evangel of violence was producing. Employers steadfastly refused to deal with the I. W. W., although they repeatedly asserted they were willing to negotiate with their employees themselves. After three months of strike and turmoil the mayor of Paterson had said: "The fight which Paterson is making is the fight of the nation. Their agitation has no other object in view but to establish a reign of terror throughout the United States." A large number of thoughtful people all over the land were beginning to share this view.

In New York City a new sort of agitation was devised in the winter of 1913–14 under the captaincy of a young man who quite suddenly found himself widely advertised. Frank Tannenbaum organized an "army of the unemployed," commandeered Rutgers Square as a rendezvous, Fifth Avenue as a parade ground, and churches and parish houses as forts and commissaries. Several of the churches were voluntarily opened to them, but other churches they attempted to enter by storm. In March, 1914, Tannenbaum led several score into the church of St. Alphonsus while mass was being celebrated. Many arrests followed this bold attempt to emulate the French Revolutionists. Though sympathizers raised $7500 bail for the ringleader, Tannenbaum loyally refused to accept it as long as any of his "army" remained in jail. Squads of his men entered restaurants, ate their fill, refused to pay, and then found their way to the workhouse. So for several months a handful of unemployed, some of them professional unemployed, held the headlines of the metropolitan papers, rallied to their defense sentimental social sympathizers, and succeeded in calling the attention of the public to a serious industrial condition.

At Granite City, Illinois, another instance of unrest occurred when several thousand laborers in the steel mills, mostly Roumanians and Bulgarians, demanded an increase in wages. When the whistle blew on the appointed morning, they gathered at the gates, refused to enter, and continued to shout "Two dollars a day!" Though the manager feared violence and posted guards, no violence was offered. Suddenly at the end of two hours the men quietly resumed their work, and the management believed the trouble was over. But for several successive mornings this maneuver was repeated. Strike breakers were then sent for. For a week, however, the work went forward as usual. The order for strike breakers was countermanded. Then came a continued repetition of the early morning strikes until the company gave way.

Nor were the subtler methods of sabotage forgotten in these demonstrations. From many places came reports of emery dust in the gearings of expensive machines. Men boasted of powdered soap emptied into water tanks that fed boilers, of kerosene applied to belting, of railroad switches that had been tampered with. With these and many similar examples before them, the public became convinced that the mere arresting of a few leaders was futile. A mass meeting at Ipswich, Massachusetts, in 1913, declared, as its principle of action, "We have got to meet force with force," and then threatened to run the entire local I. W. W. group out of town. In many towns vigilance committees acted as eyes, ears, and hands for the community. When the community refused to remain neutral, the contest assumed a different aspect and easily became a feud between a small group of militants and the general public.

In the West this contest assumed its most aggressive form. At Spokane, in 1910, the jail was soon filled, and sixty prisoners went on a hunger strike which cost several lives. In the lumber mills of Aberdeen, South Dakota, explosions and riots occurred. In Hoquiam, Washington, a twelve-foot stockade surmounted by barbed wire entanglements failed to protect the mills from the assaults of strikers. At Gray's Harbor, Washington, a citizens' committee cut the electric light wires to darken the meeting place of the I. W. W. and then used axe handles and wagon spokes to drive the members out of town. At Everett, Washington, a strike in the shingle mills led to the expulsion of the I. W. W. The leaders then called for volunteers to invade Everett, and several hundred members sailed from Seattle. They were met at the dock, however, by a large committee of citizens and were informed by the sheriff that they would not be allowed to land. After some parley, the invaders opened fire, and in the course of the shooting that followed the sheriff was seriously wounded, five persons were killed, and many were injured. The boat and its small invading army then returned to Seattle without making a landing at Everett.

The I. W. W. found an excuse for their riotous action in the refusal of communities to permit them to speak in the streets and public places. This, they claimed, was an invasion of their constitutional right of free speech. The experience of San Diego serves as an example of their "free speech" campaigns. In 1910, I. W. W. agitators began to hold public meetings in the streets, in the course of which their language increased in ferocity until the indignation of the community was aroused. An ordinance was then passed by the city council prohibiting street speaking within the congested portions of the city, but allowing street meetings in other parts of the city if a permit from the police department were first obtained. There was, however, no law requiring the issue of such a permit, and none was granted to the agitators. This restriction of their liberties greatly incensed the agitators, who at once raised the cry of "free speech" and began to hold meetings in defiance of the ordinance. The jail was soon glutted with these apostles of riotous speaking. In order to delay the dispatch of the court's overcrowded calendar, every one demanded a jury trial. The mayor of the town then received a telegram from the general secretary of the organization which disclosed their tactics: "This fight will be continued until free speech is established in San Diego if it takes twenty thousand members and twenty years to do so." The national membership of the I. W. W. had been drafted as an invading army, to be a constant irritation to the city until it surrendered. The police asserted that "there are bodies of men leaving all parts of the country for San Diego" for the purpose of defying the city authorities and overwhelming its municipal machinery. A committee of vigilantes armed with "revolvers, knives, night-sticks, black jacks, and black snakes," supported by the local press and commercial bodies, undertook to run the unwelcome guests out of town. That this was not done gently is clearly disclosed by subsequent official evidence. Culprits were loaded into auto trucks at night, taken to the county line, made to kiss the flag, sing the national anthem, run the gauntlet between rows of vigilantes provided with cudgels and, after thus proving their patriotism under duress, were told never to return.

"There is an unwritten law," one of the local papers at this time remarked, "that permits a citizen to avenge his outraged honor. There is an unwritten law that permits a community to defend itself by any means in its power, lawful or unlawful,

against any evil which the operation of the written
law is inadequate to oppose or must oppose by
slow, tedious, and unnecessarily expensive proceedings." So this municipal homeopathy of curing lawlessness with lawlessness received public sanction.

With the declaration of war against Germany in
April, 1917, hostility to the I. W. W. on the part
of the American public was intensified. The members of the organization opposed war. Their leaflet
War and the Workers, bore this legend:

> **GENERAL SHERMAN SAID
> "WAR IS HELL"**
>
> ## DON'T GO TO HELL
>
> IN ORDER TO GIVE A BUNCH OF
>
> ### PIRATICAL
> ### PLUTOCRATIC
> ### PARASITES
>
> **A BIGGER SLICE OF HEAVEN**

Soon rumors abounded that German money was
being used to aid the I. W. W. in their plots. In

Oklahoma, Texas, Illinois, Kansas, and other States, members of the organization were arrested for failure to comply with the draft law. The governors of Oregon, Washington, Montana, Idaho, and Nevada met to plan laws for suppressing the I. W. W. Similar legislation was urged upon Congress. Senator Thomas, in a report to the Senate, accused the I. W. W. of coöperating with German agents in the copper mines and harvest fields of the West by inciting the laborers to strikes and to the destruction of food and material. Popular opinion in the West inclined to the view of Senator Poindexter of Washington when he said that "most of the I. W. W. leaders are outlaws or ought to be made outlaws because of their official utterances, inflammatory literature and acts of violence." Indeed, scores of communities in 1917 took matters into their own hands. Over a thousand I. W. W. strikers in the copper mines of Bisbee, Arizona, were loaded into freight cars and shipped over the state line. In Billings, Montana, one leader was horsewhipped, and two others were hanged until they were unconscious. In Tulsa, Oklahoma, a group of seventeen members were taken from policemen, thoroughly flogged, tarred, feathered, and driven out of town by vigilantes.

The Federal Government, after an extended inquiry through the secret service, raided the Detroit headquarters of the I. W. W., where a plot to tie up lake traffic was brewing. The Chicago offices were raided some time later; over one hundred and sixty leaders of the organization from all parts of the country were indicted as a result of the examination of the wagon-load of papers and documents seized. As a result, 166 indictments were returned. Of these 99 defendants were found guilty by the trial jury, 16 were dismissed during the trial, and 51 were dismissed before the trial. In Cleveland, Buffalo, and other lake ports similar disclosures were made, and everywhere the organization fell under popular and official suspicion.

In many other portions of the country members of the _. W. W. were tried for conspiracy under the Federal espionage act. In January, 1919, a trial jury in Sacramento found 46 defendants guilty. The offense in the majority of these cases consisted in opposing military service rather than in overt acts against the Government. But in May and June, 1919, the country was startled by a series of bomb outrages aimed at the United States Attorney-General, certain Federal district judges, and other leading public personages, which were evidently the result of centralized planning and were executed by members of the I. W. W., aided very considerably by foreign Bolshevists.

In spite of its spectacular warfare and its monopoly of newspaper headlines, the I. W. W. has never been numerically strong. The first convention claimed a membership of 60,000. All told, the organization has issued over 200,000 cards since its inception, but this total never constituted its membership at any given time, for no more fluctuating group ever existed. When the I. W. W. fosters a strike of considerable proportions, the membership rapidly swells, only to shrink again when the strike is over. This temporary membership consists mostly of foreign workmen who are recent immigrants. What may be termed the permanent membership is difficult to estimate. In 1913 there were about 14,000 members. In 1917 the membership was estimated at 75,000. Though this is probably a maximum rather than an average, nevertheless the members are mostly young men whose revolutionary ardor counterbalances their want in numbers. It is, moreover, an organization that has a wide penumbra. It readily attracts the discontented, the unemployed, the man without a horizon. In an instant it can lay

a fire and put an entire police force on the *qui vive*.
The organization has always been in financial
straits. The source of its power is to be sought
elsewhere. Financially bankrupt and numerically
unstable, the I. W. W. relies upon the brazen
cupidity of its stratagems and the habitual timor-
ousness of society for its power. It is this self-
seeking disregard of constituted authority that has
given a handful of bold and crafty leaders such
prominence in the recent literature of fear. And
the members of this industrial Ku Klux Klan, these
American Bolsheviki, assume to be the "conscious
minority" which is to lead the ranks of labor into
the Canaan of industrial bliss.

CHAPTER X

LABOR AND POLITICS

IN a democracy it is possible for organized labor to extend its influence far beyond the confines of a mere trade policy. It can move the political mechanism directly in proportion to its capacity to enlist public opinion. It is not surprising, therefore, to find that labor is eager to take part in politics or that labor parties were early organized. They were, however, doomed to failure, for no workingman's party can succeed, except in isolated localities, without the coöperation of other social and political forces. Standing alone as a political entity, labor has met only rebuff and defeat at the hands of the American voter.

The earlier attempts at direct political action were local. In Philadelphia a workingman's party was organized in 1828 as a result of the disappointment of the Mechanics' Union at its failure to achieve its ambitions by strikes. At a public meeting it was resolved to support only such candidates for the legislature and city council as would pledge themselves to the interests of "the working classes." The city was organized, and a delegate convention was called which nominated a ticket of thirty candidates for city and county offices. But nineteen of these nominees were also on the Jackson ticket, and ten on the Adams ticket; and both of these parties used the legend "Working Man's Ticket," professing to favor a shorter working day. The isolated labor candidates received only from 229 to 539 votes, while the Jackson party vote ranged from 3800 to 7000 and the Adams party vote from 2500 to 3800. So that labor's first excursion into politics revealed the eagerness of the older parties to win the labor vote, and the futility of relying on a separate organization, except for propaganda purposes.

Preparatory to their next campaign, the workingmen organized political clubs in all the wards of Philadelphia. In 1829 they nominated thirty-two candidates for local offices, of whom nine received the endorsement of the Federalists and three that of the Democrats. The workingmen fared better in this election, polling nearly 2000 votes in the county and electing sixteen candidates. So encouraged were they by this success that they attempted to nominate a state ticket, but the dominant parties were too strong. In 1831 the workingmen's candidates, who were not endorsed by the older parties, received less than 400 votes in Philadelphia. After this year the party vanished.

New York also early had an illuminating experience in labor politics. In 1829 the workingmen of the city launched a political venture under the immediate leadership of an agitator by the name of Thomas Skidmore. Skidmore set forth his social panacea in a book whose elongated title betrays his secret: *The Rights of Man to Property! Being a Proposition to Make it Equal among the Adults of the Present Generation; and to Provide for its Equal Transmission to Every Individual of Each Succeeding Generation, on Arriving at the Age of Maturity.* The party manifesto began with the startling declaration that "all human society, our own as well as every other, is constructed radically wrong." The new party proposed to right this defect by an equal distribution of the land and by an elaborate system of public education. Associated with Skidmore were Robert Dale Owen and Frances Wright of the *Free Enquirer*, a paper advocating all sorts of extreme social and economic doctrines. It was

not strange, therefore, that the new party was at
once connected, in the public mind, with all the
erratic vagaries of these Apostles of Change. It
was called the "Fanny Wright ticket" and the
"Infidel Ticket." Every one forgot that it aimed
to be the workingman's ticket. The movement,
however, was supported by *The Working Man's
Advocate*, a new journal that soon reached a
wide influence.

There now appeared an eccentric Quaker, Rus-
sell Comstock by name, to center public attention
still more upon the new party. As a candidate
for the legislature, he professed an alarmingly advanced position, for he believed that the State
ought to establish free schools where handicrafts
and morals, but not religion, should be taught;
that husband and wife should be equals before the
law; that a mechanics' lien and bankruptcy law
should be passed; and that by wise graduations all
laws for the collection of debts should be repealed.
At a meeting held at the City Hall, for the further
elucidation of his "pure Republicanism," he was
greeted by a great throng but was arrested for
disturbing the peace. He received less than one
hundred and fifty votes, but his words went far to
excite, on the one hand, the interest of the laboring

classes in reform, and, on the other hand, the determination of the conservative classes to defeat "a ticket got up openly and avowedly," as one newspaper said, "in opposition to all banks, in opposition to social order, in opposition to rights of property."

Elections at this time lasted three days. On the first day there was genuine alarm at the large vote cast for "the Infidels." Thoughtful citizens were importuned to go to the polls, and on the second and third days they responded in sufficient numbers to compass the defeat of the entire ticket, excepting only one candidate for the legislature.

The Workingman's party contained too many zealots to hold together. After the election of 1829 a meeting was called to revise the party platform. The more conservative element prevailed and omitted the agrarian portions of the platform. Skidmore, who was present, attempted to protest, but his voice was drowned by the clamor of the audience. He then started a party of his own, which he called the Original Workingman's party but which became known as the Agrarian party. The majority endeavored to rectify their position in the community by an address to the people. "We take this opportunity," they said, "to aver, whatever may be said to the contrary by ignorant or designing individuals or biased presses, that we have no desire or intention of disturbing the rights of property in individuals or the public." In the meantime Robert Dale Owen and Fanny Wright organized a party of their own, endorsing an extreme form of state paternalism over children. This State Guardianship Plan, as it was called, aimed to "regenerate America in a generation" and to "make but one class out of the many that now envy and despise each other."

There were, then, three workingmen's parties in New York, none of which, however, succeeded in gaining an influential position in state politics. After 1830 all these parties disappeared, but not without leaving a legacy of valuable experience. *The Working Man's Advocate* discovered political wisdom when it confessed that "whether these measures are carried by the formation of a new party, by the reform of an old one, or by the abolishment of party altogether, is of comparative unimportance."

In New England, the workingmen's political endeavors were joined with those of the farmers under the agency of the New England Association of Farmers, Mechanics, and Workingmen. This

organization was initiated in 1830 by the workingmen of Woodstock, Vermont, and their journal, the
Working Man's Gazette, became a medium of agitation which affected all the New England manufacturing towns as well as many farming communities. "Woodstock meetings," as they were
called, were held everywhere and aroused both
workingmen and farmers to form a new political
party. *The Springfield Republican* summarized
the demands of the new party thus:

The avowed objects generally seem to be to abolish
imprisonment for debt, the abolishment of litigation,
and in lieu thereof the settlement of disputes by reference to neighbors; to establish some more equal and
universal system of public education; to diminish the
salaries and extravagance of public officers; to support
no men for offices of public trust, but farmers, mechanics, and what the party call "working men"; and to
elevate the character of this class by mental instruc-
tion and mental improvement. . . . Much is said
against the wealth and aristocracy of the land, their
influence, and the undue influence of lawyers and other
professional men. . . . The most of these objects
appear very well on paper and we believe they are
already sustained by the good sense of the people. . . .
What is most ridiculous about this party is, that in
many places where the greatest noise is made about it,
the most indolent and most worthless persons, men of
no trade or useful occupation have taken the lead.

We cannot of course answer for the character for industry of many places where this party is agitated: but we believe the great body of our own community, embracing every class and profession, may justly be called workingmen: nor do we believe enough can be found who are not such, to make even a decent party of drones.

In the early thirties many towns and cities in Massachusetts, Vermont, Maine, Connecticut, and Rhode Island elected workingmen's candidates to local offices, usually with the help of small tradespeople. In 1833 and 1834 the workingmen of Massachusetts put a state ticket in the field which polled about 2000 votes, and in Boston a workingman's party was organized, but it did not gather much momentum and soon disappeared.

These local and desultory attempts at forming a separate labor party failed as partisan movements. The labor leader proved an inefficient amateur when matched against the shrewd and experienced party manipulator; nor was there a sufficient class homogeneity to keep the labor vote together; and, even if it had so been united, there were not enough labor votes to make a majority. So the labor candidate had to rely on the good will of other classes in order to win his election. And this support was not forthcoming. Americans have, thus far, always looked with suspicion upon a party that represented primarily the interests of only one class. This tendency shows a healthy instinct founded upon the fundamental conception of society as a great unity whose life and progress depend upon the freedom of all its diverse parts.

It is not necessary to assume, as some observers have done, that these petty political excursions wrecked the labor movement of that day. It was perfectly natural that the laborer, when he awoke to the possibilities of organization and found himself possessed of unlimited political rights, should seek a speedy salvation in the ballot box. He took, by impulse, the partisan shortcut and soon found himself lost in the slough of party intrigue. On the other hand, it should not be concluded that these intermittent attempts to form labor parties were without political significance. The politician is usually blind to every need except the need of his party; and the one permanent need of his party is votes. A demand backed by reason will usually find him inert; a demand backed by votes galvanizes him into nervous attention. When, therefore, it was apparent that there was a labor vote, even though a small one, the demands of this vote were not to be ignored, especially in States where the parties were well balanced and the scale was tipped by a few hundred votes. Within a few decades after the political movement began, many States had passed lien laws, had taken active measures to establish efficient free schools, had abolished imprisonment for debt, had made legislative inquiry into factory conditions, and had recognized the ten-hour day. These had been the leading demands of organized labor, and they had been brought home to the public conscience, in part at least, by the influence of the workingmen's votes.

It was not until after the Civil War that labor achieved sufficient national homogeneity to attempt seriously the formation of a national party. In the light of later events it is interesting to sketch briefly the development of the political power of the workingman. The National Labor Union at its congress of 1866 resolved "that, so far as political action is concerned, each locality should be governed by its own policy, whether to run an independent ticket of workingmen, or to use political parties already existing, but at all events to cast no vote except for men pledged to the interests of labor." The issue then seemed clear enough. But six years later the Labor Reform party struck out on an independent course and held its first and only national convention. Seventeen States were represented.[1] The Labor party, however, had yet to learn how hardly won are independence and unity in any political organization. Rumors of pernicious intermeddling by the Democratic and Republican politicians were afloat, and it was charged that the Pennsylvania delegates had come on passes issued by the president of the Pennsylvania Railroad. Judge David Davis of Illinois, then a member of the United States Supreme Court, was nominated for President and Governor Joel Parker of New Jersey for Vice-President. Both declined, however, and Charles O'Conor of New York, the candidate of "the Straight-Out Democrats," was named for President, but no nomination was made for Vice-President. Considering the subsequent phenomenal growth of the labor vote, it is worth noting in passing that O'Conor received only 29,489 votes and that these embraced both the labor and the so-called "straight" Democratic strength.

For some years the political labor movement

[1] It is interesting to note that in this first National Labor Party Convention a motion favoring government ownership and the referendum was voted down.

lost its independent character and was absorbed
by the Greenback party which offered a meeting-
ground for discontented farmers and restless workingmen. In 1876 the party nominated for President the venerable Peter Cooper, who received
about eighty thousand votes — most of them probably cast by farmers. During this time the leaders
of the labor movement were serving a political apprenticeship and were learning the value of co-
operation. On February 22, 1878, a conference
held at Toledo, Ohio, including eight hundred
delegates from twenty-eight States, perfected an
alliance between the Labor Reform and Greenback
parties and invited all "patriotic citizens to unite
in an effort to secure financial reform and industrial
emancipation." Financial reform meant the adoption of the well-known greenback free silver policy.
Industrial emancipation involved the enactment
of an eight-hour law; the inspection of workshops,
factories, and mines; the regulation of interstate
commerce; a graduated federal income tax; the
prohibition of the importation of alien contract
labor; the forfeiture of the unused portion of the
princely land grants to railroads; and the direct
participation of the people in government. These
fundamental issues were included in the demands

of subsequent labor and populist parties, and some
of them were bequeathed to the Progressive party
of a later date. The convention was thus a forerunner of genuine reform, for its demands were
based upon industrial needs. For the moment it
made a wide popular appeal. In the state elections
of 1878 about a million votes were polled by the
party candidates. The bulk of these were farmers'
votes cast in the Middle and Far West, though in
the East, Massachusetts, Pennsylvania, New York,
Maine, and New Jersey cast a considerable vote
for the party.

With high expectations the new party entered
the campaign of 1880. It had over a dozen members in Congress, active organizations in nearly
every State, and ten thousand local clubs. General
James B. Weaver, the presidential nominee of the
party, was the first candidate to make extensive
campaign journeys into distant sections of the
country. His energetic canvass netted him only
308,578 votes, most of which came from the West.
The party was distinctly a farmers' party. In
1884, it nominated the lurid Ben Butler who had
been, according to report, "ejected from the Democratic party and booted out of the Republican."
His demagogic appeals, however, brought him not

much more than half as many votes as the party received at the preceding election, and helped to end the political career of the Greenbackers.

With the power of the farmers on the wane, the balance began to shift. There now followed a number of attempts to organize labor in the Union Labor party, the United Labor party, the Progressive Labor party, the American Reform party, and the Tax Reformers. There were still numerous farmers' organizations such as the Farmers' Alliance, the Anti-Monopolists, the Homesteaders, and others, but they were no longer the dominant force. Under the stimulus of the labor unions, delegates representing the Knights of Labor, the Grangers, the Anti-Monopolists, and other farmers' organizations, met in Cincinnati on February 22, 1887, and organized the National Union Labor party.[1] The following May the party held its only nominating convention. Alson J. Streeter of Illinois was named for President and Samuel Evans of Texas for Vice-President. The platform of the party was based upon the prevalent economic and political discontent. Farmers were overmortgaged, laborers were underpaid, and the poor were growing poorer, while the rich were daily growing richer.

[1] McKee, *National Conventions and Platforms*, p. 251.

"The paramount issues," the new party declared, "are the abolition of usury, monopoly, and trusts, and we denounce the Republican and Democratic parties for creating and perpetuating these monstrous evils."

In the meantime Henry George, whose *Progress and Poverty* had made a profound impression upon public thought, had become in 1886 a candidate for mayor of New York City, and polled the phenomenal total of 68,110 votes, while Theodore Roosevelt, the Republican candidate, received 60,435, and Abram S. Hewitt, the successful Democratic candidate, polled 90,552. The evidence of popular support which attended Henry George's brief political career was the prelude to a national effort which culminated in the formation of the United Labor party. Its platform was similar to that of the Union party, except that the single tax now made its appearance. This method contemplated the "taxation of land according to its value and not according to its area, to devote to common use and benefit those values which arise, not from the exertion of the individual, but from the growth of society," and the abolition of all taxes on industry and its products. But it was apparent from the similarity of their platforms and the geographical

distribution of their candidates that the two labor
parties were competing for the same vote. At a
conference held in Chicago to effect a union, however, the Union Labor party insisted on the complete effacement of the other ticket and the single
taxers refused to submit. In the election which
followed, the Union Labor party received about
147,000 votes, largely from the South and West
and evidently the old Greenback vote, while the
United party polled almost no votes outside of
Illinois and New York. Neither party survived
the result of this election.

In December, 1889, committees representing
the Knights of Labor and the Farmers' Alliance
met in St. Louis to come to some agreement on
political policies. Owing to the single tax predilec-
tion of the Knights, the two organizations were
unable to enter into a close union, but they nevertheless did agree that "the legislative committees
of both organizations [would] act in concert before
Congress for the purpose of securing the enactment
of laws in harmony with their demands." This
coöperation was a forerunner of the People's party
or, as it was commonly called, the Populist party,
the largest third party that had taken the field
since the Civil War. Throughout the West and the

South political conditions now were feverish. Old party majorities were overturned, and a new type of Congressman invaded Washington. When the first national convention of the People's party met in Omaha on July 2, 1892, the outlook was bright. General Weaver was nominated for President and James G. Field of Virginia for Vice-President. The platform rehabilitated Greenbackism in cogent phrases, demanded government control of railroads and telegraph and telephone systems, the reclamation of land held by corporations, an income tax, the free coinage of silver and gold "at the present legal ratio of sixteen to one," and postal savings banks. In a series of resolutions which were not a part of the platform but were nevertheless "expressive of the sentiment of this convention," the party declared itself in sympathy "with the efforts of organized workingmen to shorten the hours of labor"; it condemned "the fallacy of protecting American labor under the present system, which opens our ports to the pauper and criminal classes of the world and crowds out our wage-earners"; and it opposed the Pinkerton system of capitalistic espionage as "a menace to our liberties." The party formally declared itself to be a "union of the labor forces of the United States," for "the interests of rural and city labor are the same; their enemies identical."

These national movements prior to 1896 are not, however, an adequate index of the political strength of labor in partisan endeavor. Organized labor was more of a power in local and state elections, perhaps because in these cases its pressure was more direct, perhaps because it was unable to cope with the great national organization of the older parties. During these years of effort to gain a footing in the Federal Government, there are numerous examples of the success of the labor party in state elections. As early as 1872 the labor reformers nominated state tickets in Pennsylvania and Connecticut. In 1875 they nominated Wendell Phillips for Governor of Massachusetts. In 1878, in coalition with the Greenbackers, they elected many state officers throughout the West. Ten years later, when the Union Labor party was at its height, labor candidates were successful in several municipalities. In 1888 labor tickets were nominated in many Western States, including Colorado, Indiana, Kansas, Minnesota, Michigan, Missouri, Nebraska, Ohio, and Wisconsin. Of these Kansas cast the largest labor vote, with nearly 36,000, and Missouri came next with 15,400. In the East, however, the showing of the party in state elections was far less impressive.

In California the political labor movement achieved a singular prominence. In 1877 the labor situation in San Francisco became acute because of the prevalence of unemployment. Grumblings of dissatisfaction soon gave way to parades and informal meetings at which imported Chinese labor and the rich "nobs," the supposed dual cause of all the trouble, were denounced in lurid language. The agitation, however, was formless until the necessary leader appeared in Dennis Kearney, a native of Cork County, Ireland. For fourteen years he had been a sailor, had risen rapidly to first officer of a clipper ship, and then had settled in San Francisco as a drayman. He was temperate and industrious in his personal life, and possessed a clear eye, a penetrating voice, the vocabulary of one versed in the crude socialistic pamphlets of his day, and, in spite of certain domineering habits bred in the sailor, the winning graces of his nationality.

Kearney appeared at meetings on the vacant lots known as the "sand lots," in front of the City Hall of San Francisco, and advised the discontented ones to "wrest the government from the hands of the rich and place it in those of the people." On

September 12, 1877, he rallied a group of unemployed around him and organized the Workingman's Trade and Labor Union of San Francisco. On the 5th of October, at a great public meeting, the Workingman's party of California was formed and Kearney was elected president. The platform adopted by the party proposed to place the government in the hands of the people, to get rid of the Chinese, to destroy the money power, to "provide decently for the poor and unfortunate, the weak and the helpless," and "to elect none but competent workingmen and their friends to any office whatever. . . . When we have 10,000 members we shall have the sympathy and support of 20,000 other workingmen. This party," concluded the pronouncement, "will exhaust all peaceable means of attaining its ends, but it will not be denied justice, when it has the power to enforce it. It will encourage no riot or outrage, but it will not volunteer to repress or put down or arrest or prosecute the hungry and impatient, who manifest their hatred of the Chinamen by a crusade against 'John,' or those who employ him. Let those who raise the storm by their selfishness, suppress it themselves. If they dare raise the devil, let them meet him face to face. We will not help them."

In advocating these views, Kearney held meeting after meeting, each rhetorically more violent than the last, until on the 3d of November he was arrested. This martyrdom in the cause of labor increased his power, and when he was released he was drawn by his followers in triumph through the streets on one of his own drays. His language became more and more extreme. He bludgeoned the "thieving politicians" and the "bloodsucking capitalists," and he advocated "judicious hanging" and "discretionary shooting." The City Council passed an ordinance intended to gag him; the legislature enacted an extremely harsh riot act; a body of volunteers patrolled the streets of the city; a committee of safety was organized. On January 5, 1878, Kearney and a number of associates were indicted, arrested, and released on bail. When the trial jury acquitted Kearney, what may be called the terrorism of the movement attained its height, but it fortunately spent itself in violent adjectives.

The Workingman's party, however, elected a workingman mayor of San Francisco, joined forces with the Grangers, and elected a majority of the members of the state constitutional convention which met in Sacramento on September 28, 1878.

This was a notable triumph for a third party. The framing of a new constitution gave this coalition of farmers and workingmen an unusual opportunity to assail the evils which they declared infested the State. The instrument which they drafted bound the state legislature with numerous restrictions and made lobbying a felony; it reorganized the courts, placed innumerable limitations upon corporations, forbade the loaning of the credit or property of the State to corporations, and placed a state commission in charge of the railroads, which had been perniciously active in state politics. Alas for these visions of reform! A few years after the adoption of this new constitution by California, Hubert H. Bancroft wrote:

Those objects which it particularly aimed at, it failed to achieve. The effect upon corporations disappointed its authors and supporters. Many of them were strong enough still to defy state power and evade state laws, in protecting their interests, and this they did without scruple. The relation of capital and labor is even more strained than before the constitution was adopted. Capital soon recovered from a temporary intimidation. . . . Labor still uneasy was still subject to the inexorable law of supply and demand. Legislatures were still to be approached by agents. . . . Chinese were still employed in digging and grading. The state board of railroad Commissioners was a useless expense, . . . being as wax in the hands of the companies it was set to watch.[1]

After the collapse of the Populist party, there is to be discerned in labor politics a new departure, due primarily to the attitude of the American Federation of Labor in partisan matters, and secondarily to the rise of political socialism. A socialistic party deriving its support almost wholly from foreign-born workmen had appeared in a few of the large cities in 1877, but it was not until 1892 that a national party was organized, and not until after the collapse of Populism that it assumed some political importance.

In August, 1892, a Socialist-Labor convention which was held in New York City nominated candidates for President and Vice-President and adopted a platform that contained, besides the familiar economic demands of socialism, the rather unusual suggestion that the Presidency, Vice-Presidency, and Senate of the United States be abolished and that an executive board be established "whose members are to be elected, and may at any time be recalled, by the House of Representatives, as the only legislative body, the States and municipalities to adopt corresponding

[1] *Works* (vol. XXIV): *History of California*, vol. VII, p. 404.

amendments to their constitutions and statutes."
Under the title of the Socialist-Labor party, this
ticket polled 21,532 votes in 1892, and in 1896,
36,373 votes.

In 1897 the inevitable split occurred in the Socialist ranks. Eugene V. Debs, the radical labor leader,
who, as president of the American Railway Union,
had directed the Pullman strike and had become a
martyr to the radical cause through his imprisonment for violating the orders of a Federal Court,
organized the Social-Democratic party. In 1900
Debs was nominated for President, and Job Harri-
man, representing the older wing, for Vice-President. The ticket polled 94,864 votes. The Socialist-Labor party nominated a ticket of their own
which received only 33,432 votes. Eventually this
party shrank to a mere remnant, while the Social
Democratic party became generally known as the
Socialist party. Debs became their candidate in
three successive elections. In 1904 and 1908 his
vote hovered around 400,000. In 1910 congressional and local elections spurred the Socialists
to hope for a million votes in 1912 but they
fell somewhat short of this mark. Debs received 901,873 votes, the largest number which a
Socialist candidate has ever yet received. Benson,

the presidential candidate in 1916, received 590,-
579 votes. [1]

In the meantime, the influence of the Socialist
labor vote in particular localities vastly increased.
In 1910 Milwaukee elected a Socialist mayor by a
plurality of seven thousand, sent Victor Berger to
Washington as the first Socialist Congressman, and
elected labor-union members as five of the twelve
Socialist councilmen, thus revealing the sympathy
of the working class for the cause. On January 1,
1912, over three hundred towns and cities had one
or more Socialist officers. The estimated Socialist
vote of these localities was 1,500,000. The 1039
Socialist officers included 56 mayors, 205 aldermen
and councilmen, and 148 school officers. This was
not a sectional vote but represented New England
and the far West, the oldest commonwealths and
the newest, the North and the South, and cities filled
with foreign workingmen as well as staid towns
controlled by retired farmers and shopkeepers.

When the United States entered the Great War,
the Socialist party became a reservoir for all the
unsavory disloyalties loosened by the shock of the

[1] The Socialist vote is stated differently by McKee, *National
Conventions and Platforms.* The above figures, to 1912, are taken
from Stanwood's *History of the Presidency,* and for 1912 and 1916
from the *World Almanac.*

great conflict. Pacifists and pro-Germans found a common refuge under its red banner. In the New York mayoralty elections in 1917 these Socialists cast nearly one-fourth of the votes, and in the Wisconsin senatorial election in 1918 Victor Berger, their standard-bearer, swept Milwaukee, carried seven counties, and polled over one hundred thousand votes. On the other hand, a large number of American Socialists, under the leadership of William English Walling and John Spargo, vigorously espoused the national cause and subordinated their economic and political theories to their loyalty.

The Socialists have repeatedly attempted to make official inroads upon organized labor. They have the sympathy of the I. W. W., the remnant of the Knights of Labor, and the more radical trades unions, but from the American Federation of Labor they have met only rebuff. A number of state federations, especially in the Middle West, not a few city centrals, and some sixteen national unions, have officially approved of the Socialist programme, but the Federation has consistently refused such an endorsement.

The political tactics assumed by the Federation discountenance a distinct labor party movement, as long as the old parties are willing to subserve the ends of the unions. This self-restraint does not mean that the Federation is not "in politics." On the contrary, it is constantly vigilant and aggressive and it engages every year in political maneuvers without, however, having a partisan organization of its own. At its annual conventions it has time and again urged local and state branches to scrutinize the records of legislative candidates and to see that only friends of union labor receive the union laborer's ballot. In 1897 it "firmly and unequivocally" favored "the independent use of the ballot by trade unionists and workmen united regardless of party, that we may elect men from our own ranks to write new laws and administer them along lines laid down in the legislative demands of the American Federation of Labor and at the same time secure an impartial judiciary that will not govern us by arbitrary injunctions of the courts, nor act as the pliant tool of corporate wealth." And in 1906 it determined, first, to defeat all candidates who are either hostile or indifferent to labor's demands; second, if neither party names such candidates, then to make independent labor nominations; third, in every instance to support "the men who have shown themselves to be friendly to labor."

With great astuteness, perseverance, and alert-
ness, the Federation has pursued this method to its
uttermost possibilities. In Washington it has met
with singular success, reaching a high-water mark
in the first Wilson Administration, with the passage of the Clayton bill and the eight-hour railroad
bill. After this action, a great New York daily
lamented that "Congress is a subordinate branch
of the American Federation of Labor. . . . The
unsleeping watchmen of organized labor know how
intrepid most Congressmen are when threatened
with the 'labor vote.' The American laborites don't
have to send men to Congress as their British
brethren do to the House of Commons. From the
galleries they watch the proceedings. They are
mighty in committee rooms. They reason with the
recalcitrant. They fight opponents in their Congress
districts. There are no abler or more potent politicians than the labor leaders out of Congress. Why
should rulers like Mr. Gompers and Mr. Furuseth[1]
go to Congress? They are a Super-Congress."

Many Congressmen have felt the retaliatory
power of the Federation. Even such powerful
leaders as Congressman Littlefield of Maine and

---

[1] Andrew Furuseth, the president of the Seamen's Union and
reputed author of the Seaman's Act of 1915.

Speaker Cannon were compelled to exert their ut-
most to overcome union opposition. The Federation has been active in seating union men in Congress. In 1908 there were six union members in
the House; in 1910 there were ten; in 1912 there
were seventeen. The Secretary of Labor himself
holds a union card. Nor has the Federation shrunk
from active participation in the presidential lists.
It bitterly opposed President Roosevelt when he
espoused the open shop in the Government Printing Office; and in 1908 it openly espoused the
Democratic ticket.

In thus maintaining a sort of grand partisan
neutrality, the Federation not only holds in numerous instances the balance of power but it makes
party fealty its slave and avoids the costly luxury
of maintaining a separate national organization
of its own. The all-seeing lobby which it maintains
at Washington is a prototype of what one may discern in most state capitals when the legislature is
in session. The legislative programmes adopted by
the various state labor bodies are metamorphosed
into demands, and well organized committees are
present to coöperate with the labor members
who sit in the legislature. The unions, through
their steering committee, select with caution the

members who are to introduce the labor bills and watch paternally over every stage in the progress of a measure.

Most of this legislative output has been strictly protective of union interests. Labor, like all other interests that aim to use the power of government, has not been wholly altruistic in its motives, especially since in recent years it has found itself matched against such powerful organizations of employers as the Manufacturers' Association, the National Erectors' Association, and the Metal Trades Association. In fact, in nearly every important industry the employers have organized for defensive and offensive purposes. These organizations match committee with committee, lobby with lobby, add espionage to open warfare, and issue effective literature in behalf of their open shop propaganda.

The voluminous labor codes of such great manufacturing communities as Massachusetts, New York, Pennsylvania, and Illinois, reflect a new and enlarged conception of the modern State. Labor has generally favored measures that extend the inquisitional and regulative functions of the State, excepting where this extension seemed to interfere with the autonomy of labor itself. Workshops, mines, factories, and other places of employment are now minutely inspected, and innumerable sanitary and safety provisions are enforced. A workman's compensation law removes from the employee's mind his anxiety for the fate of his family if he should be disabled. The labor contract, long extolled as the ægis of economic liberty, is no longer free from state vigilance. The time and method of paying wages are ordered by the State, and in certain industries the hours of labor are fixed by law. Women and children are the special protégés of this new State, and great care is taken that they shall be engaged only in employment suitable to their strength and under an environment that will not ruin their health.

The growing social control of the individual is significant, for it is not only the immediate conditions of labor that have come under public surveillance. Where and how the workman lives is no longer a matter of indifference to the public, nor what sort of schooling his children get, what games they play, and what motion pictures they see. The city, in coöperation with the State, now provides nurses, dentists, oculists, and surgeons, as well as teachers for the children. This local paternalism increases yearly in its solicitude and receives the eager sanction of the labor members of city councils. The State has also set up elaborate machinery for observing all phases of the labor situation and for gathering statistics and other information that should be helpful in framing labor laws, and has also established state employment agencies and boards of conciliation and arbitration.

This machinery of mediation is significant not because of what it has already accomplished but as evidence of the realization on the part of the State that labor disputes are not merely the concern of the two parties to the labor contract. Society has finally come to realize that, in the complex of the modern State, it also is vitally concerned, and, in despair at thousands of strikes every year, with their wastage and their aftermath of bitterness, it has attempted to interpose its good offices as mediator.

The modern labor laws cannot be credited, however, to labor activity alone. The new social atmosphere has provided a congenial *milieu* for this vast extension of state functions. The philanthropist, the statistician, and the sociologist have become potent allies of the labor-legislator; and such non-labor organizations, as the American Association for Labor Legislation, have added their momentum to the movement. New ideals of social coöperation have been established, and new conceptions of the responsibilities of private ownership have been evolved.

While labor organizations have succeeded rather readily in bending the legislative power to their wishes, the military arm of the executive and the judiciary which ultimately enforce the command of the State have been beyond their reach. To bend these branches of the government to its will, organized labor has fought a persistent and aggressive warfare. Decisions of the courts which do not sustain union contentions are received with great disfavor. The open shop decisions of the United States Supreme Court are characterized as unfair and partisan and are vigorously opposed in all the labor journals. It is not, however, until the sanction of public opinion eventually backs the attitude of the unions that the laws and their interpretation can conform entirely to the desires of labor.

The chief grievance of organized labor against the courts is their use of the injunction to prevent boycotts and strikes. "Government by injunction" is the complaint of the unions and it is based upon the common, even reckless, use of a writ which was in origin and intent a high and rarely used prerogative of the Court of Chancery. What was in early times a powerful weapon in the hands of the Crown against riotous assemblies and threatened lawlessness was invoked in 1868 by an English court as a remedy against industrial disturbances.[1] Since the Civil War the American courts in rapidly increasing numbers have used this weapon, and the Damascus blade of equity has been transformed into a bludgeon in the hands even of magistrates of inferior courts.

The prime objection which labor urges against this use of the injunction is that it deprives the defendant of a jury trial when his liberty is at stake. The unions have always insisted that the law should be so modified that this right would accompany all injunctions growing out of labor disputes. Such a denatured injunction, however, would defeat the purpose of the writ; but the union leader maintains, on the other hand, that he is placed unfairly at a disadvantage, when an employer can command for his own aid in an industrial dispute the swift and sure arm of a law originally intended for a very different purpose. The imprisonment of Debs during the Pullman strike for disobeying a Federal injunction brought the issue vividly before

[1] Springfield Spinning Company *vs.* Riley, L. R. 6 Eq. 551.

the public; and the sentencing of Gompers, Mitchell, and Morrison to prison terms for violating the Buck's Stove injunction produced new waves of popular protest. Occasional dissenting opinions by judges and the gradual conviction of lawyers and of society that some other tribunal than a court of equity or even a court of law would be more suitable for the settling of labor disputes is indicative of the change ultimately to be wrought in practice.

The unions are also violently opposed to the use of military power by the State during strikes. Not only can the militia be called out to enforce the mandates of the State but whenever Federal interference is justified the United States troops may be sent to the scene of turmoil. After the period of great labor troubles culminating in the Pullman strike, many States reorganized their militia into national guards. The armories built for the accommodation of the guard were called by the unions "plutocracy's bastiles," and the mounted State constabulary organized in 1906 by Pennsylvania were at once dubbed "American Cossacks." Several States following the example of Pennsylvania have encountered the bitterest hostility on the part of the labor unions. Already opposition

to the militia has proceeded so far that some unions have forbidden their members to perform militia service when called to do strike duty, and the
military readjustments involved in the Great War
have profoundly affected the relation of the State
to organized labor. Following the signing of the
armistice, a movement for the organization of an
American Labor party patterned after the British
Labour party gained rapid momentum, especially
in New York and Chicago. A platform of fourteen
points was formulated at a general conference of
the leaders, and provisional organizations were perfected in a number of cities. What power this
latest attempt to enlist labor in partisan politics
will assume is problematical. It is obviously in-
spired by European experiences and promulgated
by socialistic propaganda. It has not succeeded in
invading the American Federation of Labor, which
did not formally endorse the movement at its Annual Convention in 1919. Gompers, in an intimate and moving speech, told a group of labor leaders gathered in New York on December 9, 1918,
that "the organization of a political party would
simply mean the dividing of the activities and allegiance of the men and women of labor between
two bodies, such as would often come in conflict."

Under present conditions, it would appear that no Labor party could succeed in the United States without the coöperation of the American Federation of Labor.

The relation between the American Federation of Labor and the socialistic and political labor movements, as well as the monopolistic eagerness of the socialists to absorb these activities, is clearly indicated in Gompers's narrative of his experiences as an American labor representative at the London Conference of 1918. The following paragraphs are significant:

When the Inter-Allied Labor Conference opened in London, on September 17th, early in the morning, there were sent over to my room at the hotel cards which were intended to be the credential cards for our delegation to sign and hand in as our credentials. The card read something like this: "The undersigned is a duly accredited delegate to the Inter-Allied Socialist Conference to be held at London," etc., and giving the dates.

I refused to sign my name, or permit my name to be put upon any card of that character. My associates were as indignant as I was and refused to sign any such credential. We went to the hall where the conference was to be held. There was a young lady at the door. When we made an effort to enter she asked for our cards. We said we had no cards to present. "Well," the answer came, "you cannot be admitted." We replied, "That may be true — we cannot be admitted — but we will not sign any such card. We have our credentials written out, signed, and sealed and will present them to any committee of the conference for scrutiny and recommendation, but we are not going to sign such a card."

Mr. Charles Bowerman, Secretary of the Parliamentary Committee of the British Trade Union Congress, at that moment emerged from the door. He asked why we had not entered. I told him the situation, and he persuaded the young lady to permit us to pass in. We entered the hall and presented our credentials. Mr. James Sexton, officer and representative of the Docker's Union of Liverpool, arose and called the attention of the Conference to this situation, and declared that the American Federation of Labor delegates refused to sign any such document. He said it was not an Inter-Allied *Socialist* Conference, but an Inter-Allied Socialist *and Labor* Conference.

Mr. Arthur Henderson, of the Labor Party, made an explanation something to this effect, if my memory serves me: "It is really regrettable that such an error should have been made. It was due to the fact that the old card of credentials which has been used in former conferences was sent to the printer, no one paying any attention to it, thinking it was all right."

I want to call your attention to the significance of that explanation, that is, that the trade union movement of Great Britain was represented at these former conferences, but at this conference the importance of

Labor was regarded as so insignificant that everybody took it for granted that it was perfectly all right to have the credential card read "Inter-Allied Socialist Conference" and with the omission of this more important term, "Labor."[1]

As one looks back upon the history of the workingman, one finds something impressive, even majestic, in the rise of the fourth estate from a humble place to one of power in this democratic nation. In this rise of fortune the laborer's union has unquestionably been a moving force, perhaps even the leading cause. At least this homogeneous mass of workingmen, guided by self-developed leadership, has aroused society to safeguard more carefully the individual needs of all its parts. Labor has awakened the state to a sense of responsibility for its great sins of neglect and has made it conscious of its social duties. Labor, like other elements of society, has often been selfish, narrow, vindictive; but it has also shown itself earnest and constructive. The conservative trades union, at the hour of this writing, stands as a bulwark between that amorphous, inefficient, irresponsible Socialism which has made Russia a lurid warning and Prussia a word of scorn, and that rational

[1] *American Federationist*, January, 1919, pp. 40–41.

social ideal which is founded upon the conviction that society is ultimately an organic spiritual unity, the blending of a thousand diverse interests whose justly combined labors and harmonized talents create civilization and develop culture.

BIBLIOGRAPHICAL NOTE

WHILE there is a vast amount of writing on the labor problem, there are very few works on the history of labor organizations in the United States. The main reliance for the earlier period, in the foregoing pages, has been the *Documentary History of American Industrial Society*, edited by John R. Commons, 10 vols. (1910). The *History of Labour in the United States*, 2 vols. (1918), which he published with associates, is the most convenient and complete compilation that has yet appeared and contains a large mass of historical material on the labor question.

The following works are devoted to discussions of various phases of the history of American labor and industry:

T. S. Adams and Helen L. Sumner, *Labor Problems* (1905). Contains several refreshing chapters on labor organizations.

F. T. Carlton, *The History and Problem of Organized Labor* (1911). A succinct discussion of union problems.

R. T. Ely, *The Labor Movement in America* (1886). Though one of the earliest American works on the subject, it remains indispensable.

G. G. Groat, *An Introduction to the Study of Organized Labor in America* (1916). A useful and up-to-date compendium.

R. F. Hoxie, *Trade Unionism in the United States* (1917). A suggestive study of the philosophy of unionism.

J. R. Commons (Ed.), *Trade Unionism and Labor Problems* (1905).

J. H. Hollander and G. E. Barnett (Eds.), *Studies in American Trade Unionism* (1905). These two volumes are collections of contemporary studies of many phases of organized labor by numerous scholars. They are not historical.

The *Report of the Industrial Commission*, vol. XVII (1901) provides the most complete analysis of trade-union policies and also contains valuable historical summaries of many unions.

G. E. McNeill (Ed.), *The Labor Movement: the Problem of Today* (1892). This collection contains historical sketches of the organizations of the greater labor groups and of the development of the more important issues espoused by them. For many years it was the most comprehensive historical work on American unionism, and it remains a necessary source of information to the student of trades union history.

J. G. Brissenden, *The Launching of the Industrial Workers of the World* (1913). An account of the origin of the I. W. W.

J. G. Brooks, *American Syndicalism: the I. W. W.* (1913).

John Mitchell, *Organized Labor* (1903). A suggestive exposition of the principles of Unionism by a distinguished labor leader. It contains only a limited amount of historical matter.

T. V. Powderly, *Thirty Years of Labor* (1889.) A history of the Knights of Labor from a personal viewpoint.

E. L. Bogart, *The Economic History of the United States* (rev. ed., 1918). A concise and clear account of our economic development.

R. T. Ely, *Evolution of Industrial Society* (1903).

Carroll D. Wright, *The Industrial Evolution of the United States* (1895).

G. S. Callender, *Selections from the Economic History of the United States* (1909). A collection of readings. The brief introductory essays to each chapter give a succinct account of American industrial development to 1860.

INDEX

Aberdeen (S. D.), I. W. W. in, 212

Adamson Law (eight-hour railroad law), 133 (note), 160, 164–66, 247

Agrarian party, 224

Akron (O.), strike in rubber works, 206–07

Albany, trade unions in, 34

Albany Mechanical Society (1801), 22

Allegheny City, ten-hour controversy in cotton mills, 54

Amalgamated Association of Iron and Steel Workers, 126

Amalgamated Labor Union, 88

Amalgamated Wood Workers' Association, 109

Amboy (Ill.), Conductors' Union organized (1868), 150

American Alliance for Labor and Democracy, 101–02

American Association for Labor Legislation, 251

"American Cossacks," 254

American Federation of Labor, suggested at Terre Haute (1881), 88; established (1886), 89; growth, 89–90; organization, 90–93, 112; Gompers and, 94 *et seq.*; financial policy, 97; and Great War, 100 *et seq.*; and labor readjustment, 107; attitude toward Socialism, 108, 111, 245, 256; tendency toward amalgamating allied trades, 109–10; and un-

skilled labor, 109; importance, 110–11; Mitchell and, 128; and Brotherhood of Locomotive Engineers, 133 (note); and Buck's Stove and Range Company boycott, 181; and Danbury Hatters' case, 184; and I. W. W., 194; and Lawrence mill workers, 203; and politics, 242, 245–46, 256; influences legislation, 246–52; and American Labor party movement, 255–56

American Federationist, organ of American Federation of Labor, 92, 181, 195

American Labor party, movement for forming, 255

American Newspaper Publishers Association, 169

American Railway Union, and strikes, 158, 159; Debs president of, 243

Anthracite Coal Strike (1902), 113, 129–30, 174; Commission cross-examines Mitchell, 130 (note)

Anti-Boycott Association, 180

Anti-Monopolist party, 233

Arbitration, 85–86; law providing for settlement of railway disputes (1888), 85; in Anthracite Coal Strike, 129–30; Board to deal with railway problems (1912), 146–50; Erdman Act (1898), 146, 162; Federal legislation